Illuminate
Publishing

AQA
Media Studies

for A Level Year 1 & AS

Revision Guide

Stephanie Hendry

Published in 2019 by Illuminate Publishing Ltd,
PO Box 1160, Cheltenham, Gloucestershire GL50 9RW

Orders: Please visit www.illuminatepublishing.com
or email sales@illuminatepublishing.com

British Library Cataloguing-in-Publication Data

A catalogue record for this book is available from the
British Library

ISBN 978-1-911208-86-0

Printed in the UK by Cambrian Printers, Aberystwyth

04.19

The publisher's policy is to use papers that are
natural, renewable and recyclable products made
from wood grown in sustainable forests. The
logging and manufacturing processes are expected
to conform to the environmental regulations of the
country of origin.

Editor: Dawn Booth

Design and layout: Jon Fletcher

Cover design: Nigel Harriss

Cover image: © Shutterstock / Dinga

Author's acknowledgments
Many thanks to A Level students past and present who
have taught me a lot about the media over the years.
Specific thanks to Rebecca Wilson and Jess Hilton
for their comments and thoughts on the revision
activities. Also, many thanks to Damien for his support,
patience and willingness to discuss and debate.

Contents

Photo acknowledgements

p1 © Shutterstock / Dinga; p5 Monkey Business Images; p7 Happy Stock Photo; p8 (top) Monster Ztudio; p8 (bottom) Solis Images; p9 Maria Symchych; p10 A Star is Born / Official Trailer 1; p11 Hunger Games; p12 (top right) Dragon Images; p12 (middle right) Yulia Reznikov / Shutterstock.com; p12 (bottom right) Poprotskly Aleaxey; p12 (middle left to right) Goran Bogicevic; TDKvisuals; susana valera; Sahacha Nilkumhang; p12 (bottom) Alexi Lubomirski / GQ © The Condé Nast Publications Ltd; p13 (bottom right) Courtesy of Men's Health / Hearst; p15 New Jaguar XJ 2013 Ultimate Commercial Your World, Reflected Carjam TV HD Car TV Show / YouTube; p16 David Beckham Making of Breitling Campaign / Airborne-Films / YouTube; p18 Maurice Savage / Alamy Stock Photo; p19 Twocoms / Shutterstock.com; p20 ducu59cs; p21 Lifestyle pictures / Alamy Stock Photo; p22 (left) AF archive / Alamy Stock Photo; p22 (right) Pictorial Press Ltd / Alamy Stock Photo; p25 The Killing; p27 Sferdon; p28 (top) Moviestore Collection Ltd / Alamy Stock Photo; p28 (bottom) The Killing; p31 Freedomz; p33 KennyK.com; p35 (top) William Perugini; p35 (middle) Followtheflow; p35 (bottom) Common - Letter to the Free ft. Bilal / thinkcommon / YouTube; p36 The Missing; p37 (top) Manny MUA; p37 (bottom) Courtesy of Men's Health / Hearst; p39 Rawpixel.com; p40 quinky; p42 Mary_ART_S;

p43 Syda Productions; p44 Courtesy Psychologies Magazine; p46 (left) Love Island; p46 (right) Dior; p49 Goncharov/Artern; p51 (top) Sergey91988; p51 (bottom) Lutsenko_Oleksandr / Shutterstock.com; p54 sdecoret; p55 (top) Courtesy of IPSO; p55 (middle) Ofcom; p55 (bottom) PEGI; p57 Pavie Burgarski; p58 Common - Letter to the Free ft. Bilal / thinkcommon / YouTube; p59 wavebreakmedia; p60 That Boss Life Pt. 1 ft. MannyMua and Mekeupshayla / New Big Shot Mascara / maybellinewyork / YouTube; p61 That Boss Life Pt. 1 ft. MannyMua and Mekeupshayla / New Big Shot Mascara / maybellinewyork / YouTube; p64 (top) Thomson Holidays; p64 (bottom) Tesco; p65 AVON TV Advert / Big & Extreme Mascara / Avon UK / YouTube; p66 (left) Vintage Maybelline Commercials / Down To Girl / YouTube; p66 (right) That Boss Life Pt. 1 ft. MannyMua and Mekeupshayla / New Big Shot Mascara / maybellinewyork / YouTube; p67 (all) That Boss Life Pt. 1 ft. MannyMua and Mekeupshayla / New Big Shot Mascara / maybellinewyork / YouTube; p68 That Boss Life Pt. 1 ft. MannyMua and Mekeupshayla / New Big Shot Mascara / maybellinewyork / YouTube; p69 That Boss Life Pt. 1 ft. MannyMua and Mekeupshayla / New Big Shot Mascara / maybellinewyork / YouTube; p70 That Boss Life Pt. 1 ft. MannyMua and Mekeupshayla / New Big Shot Mascara / maybellinewyork / YouTube;

p71 (both) That Boss Life Pt. 1 ft. MannyMua and Mekeupshayla / New Big Shot Mascara / maybellinewyork / YouTube; p72 Deutschland 83; p73 Deutschland 83; p74 (top) Deutschland 83; p74 (bottom) Deutschland 83; p75 Deutschland 83; p77 (top) UFA; p77 (middle) RTL; p77 (bottom) Walter Presents; p79 Channel Four; p81 Deutschland 83; p84 Guardian website; p86 Laura Deschner / Sundance TV / Kobal / REX / Shutterstock; p88 Rose Carson / Shutterstock.com; p87 Hidden Figures; p89 Rose Carson / Shutterstock; p90 Hidden Figures; p92 (top) 20th Century Fox; p92 (bottom) Faiz Zaki / Shutterstock.com; p93 Ververidis Vasilis; p95 Hidden Figures; p96 ZUMA Press, Inc. / Alamy Stock Photo; p98 The i; p100 Lawrey; p101 A_Lesik; p102 Source Statistica 2019; p103 (left) CBW / Alamy Stock Photo; p103 (right) CBW / Alamy Stock Photo; p106 (all) The i; p110 (left) Marco Iacobucci EPP; p110 (middle) Danel M Ernst; p110 (right) Joaquin Ossorio Castillo; p113 (top) Krafted; p113 (bottom) Courtesy YouGov; p120 (top) Car; Vam Vecjtem / Creative commons; p120 (bottom) dpa picture alliance / Alamy Stock Photo; p126 Granger / REX / Shutterstock; p128 (all top) Public domain; p128 (bottom) The War of the Worlds Mass Panic (That Never Happened) / Today I Found Out / YouTube

How to use this book

Welcome to the *AQA Media Studies for A Level Year 1 & AS Revision Guide*.

This guide aims to help with revising and preparing for the AS Media Studies examination. AS Media Studies is a standalone qualification, usually taken over one academic year.

There are two assessments that you will need to complete for AS Media Studies:

- **The non-examined assessment (NEA):** a practical production task based on briefs published by the awarding body. Advice and guidance for the NEA can be found in the *Year 1 & AS Media Studies* student book.
- **The exam:** a 2-hour examination paper that you will take at the end of the academic year.

This revision guide focuses on the two main areas that you will be assessed on: the **theoretical framework** and the **close study products** (CSPs). You will find detailed information on the theories and some of the CSPs in the Year 1 & AS Media Studies student book. You can use the student book alongside this revision guide to help you prepare for the examination.

The examination assesses your knowledge and understanding of the **theoretical framework**, which includes:

- ideas related to **media language** (including genre and narrative)
- ideas related to **media representations**
- ideas related to **media audiences**
- ideas related to **media industries**.

The specifics of the ideas you will need to be familiar with are detailed in the specification and will also be discussed in **Chapters 1, 2 and 3** of this book. These chapters will also offer revision strategies to help you revise and prepare your knowledge of the framework.

In order to demonstrate your knowledge and understanding of the theoretical framework, you will be asked to discuss and offer examples from the **close study products** identified by the exam board.

Close study products are named CSPs that cover each of the nine media forms. Some of the CSPs need to be studied using one or two areas of the framework. These are called **targeted CSPs**. Other CSPs need to be studied using all four areas of the framework. These are called the **in depth CSPs**. During your year of study, you will need to become familiar with the following **media forms**:

1 Gaming
2 Magazines
3 Advertising and marketing
4 Television
5 Music video
6 Film
7 Radio
8 Newspapers
9 Online, social and participatory media.

As of September 2018, the specific CSPs you need to be familiar with are:

The targeted CSPs:

- **to be studied with a focus on media language and media representations**
  - Gaming: Tomb Raider: Anniversary.
  - Magazines: *Men's Health*.
  - *Advertising and marketing: Maybelline: That Boss Life part 1.*
- **to be studied with a focus on media audiences and media industries**
  - Television: *Deutschland 83*, *The Missing* or *The Killing* (only one television CSP needs to be studied).
  - Music video: Common: *Letter to the Free*.
- **to be studied with a focus on industry only**
  - Film: *Hidden Figures*.

In depth CSPs:

- **to be studied with a focus on all areas of the theoretical framework**
  - Radio: *The War of the Worlds* (1936).
  - Newspapers: the *i*.
  - Online, social and participatory media: TeenVogue.com.

Chapters 4 and 5 of this book will look at selected CSPs and offer revision ideas to help you prepare them in ways that meet the examination requirements. Information on all the CSPs is offered when this book is used in conjunction with the AS and A level student books in the following ways:

Year 1 & AS book	Year 2 & A2 book	Year 1 & AS Revision Guide
Men's Health	The Killing (as an in depth, non-English language CSP)	Maybelline: That Boss Life part 1
TeenVogue.com	Tomb Raider: Anniversary (as an in depth CSP)	Deutschland 83
The Missing	Common: Letter to the Free	Hidden Figures
		The War of the Worlds
		The i

It is important to remember that although the AS CSPs are also A level CSPs, the way they are discussed may differ.

The AS Media Studies examination will ask you to discuss an 'unseen', non-CSP media product that will be included with the examination paper. This will be a print-based media product that you will not have prepared in advance of the exam. It will be in Section A of the examination and be used to assess your ability to use the theoretical framework and apply the ideas and concepts to any media product rather than one you have studied in class. In **Chapters 1, 2 and 3** different media products, along with CSPs, will be used as examples to demonstrate how the ideas can be used to discuss non-CSP products.

Initial tips for revision

Two things are assessed in all parts of the examination: knowledge and understanding.

Knowledge

For a full Glossary see pages 252–261 of the Year 1 & AS student book.

Sometimes, studying media feels like learning a new language. There are lots of specialised terms that need to be memorised and you may be asked to provide definitions or explanations of these terms in the examination or to recognise their correct use in sentences. As with any other language, the keys to remembering a vocabulary are repetition and use. You can memorise terms and what they mean by 'rote' – by memorising and repeating the terms, perhaps using flashcards to help you remember what each word means. There is nothing wrong with this approach and you will see later that each area of the framework has its own 'glossary of terms' that need to be remembered for the examination. The crucial terms you need to know are listed in Chapters 1, 2 and 3, and you will practise applying the terms and ideas in Chapters 4 and 5.

Similarly, you need to know (in some detail) the CSPs you have studied. This means that you need to remember certain key facts about each CSP (for example, who the publisher of TeenVogue.com is). You also need to remember specific details about the content of CSPs. This is especially true of those studied using media language and media representation ideas, but examples from the products are often needed to support ideas about audience and industry too. So, as their name suggests, you will need to closely study each CSP. You should be able to offer specific examples of layout, page design, and image and language choice when discussing *Men's Health* magazine. Your study of *Hidden Figures* from an industry perspective should include specific information about, for example, some of the advertising and marketing products created for the film (the trailer, posters, adverts, etc.). When discussing *The War of the Worlds*, you should be able to mention details about the audio effects used to tell the story to the audience, and when discussing the way *Letter to the Free* might appeal to its audience, details about the framing of shots and/or the use of the camera should be used. To do this means that you will need to watch, listen to or read each CSP many times during the year and then again as you prepare for the examination. You should feel confident in your knowledge of all nine media products.

Gaining the knowledge required to do well in a Media Studies examination is normally time-consuming. You can save time if you build your knowledge of the theoretical framework by using the theoretical terms to think about and discuss each CSP in detail rather than treat theory and CSPs as two separate things. It is better to approach gaining knowledge as something that you build on as the course progresses. It's not something that can be 'crammed' in a couple of weeks before the examination. If you wait until revision time to become familiar with the products and ideas studied throughout the year, you may find you don't have enough time left to focus on extending and applying your knowledge into an understanding of media concepts, theories and ideas. However, knowledge is only the start of the process of exam preparation, as the examination will ask you to show that you understand what you have learned.

Understanding

Knowing how an establishing shot is filmed is one thing. Understanding why it is used or what effect it has is more complex. The examination will want you to show that you not only know something but that you also understand it. Understanding cannot be revised using flashcards, etc. Understanding comes from considering ideas, challenging them and then contextualising them. For example, the establishing shot used towards the end of *Letter to the Free* relocates the audience from the prison setting of the video to a rural landscape. This shot has not been chosen for the same reason as the establishing shots of the different locations in *The Killing*, where this media language choice is used to identify where the action is taking place. The fundamental reason for an establishing shot is always the same and can be learned, but understanding the meaning of the shot in the context of this music video requires more detailed knowledge and understanding of the messages and ideas being communicated by the video as a whole.

Understanding often requires you to consider more than one idea at the same time and to consider the way things combine and work together, or against each other. Knowing how narrative works is relatively straightforward, but understanding how Vin Diesel is offered as a 'reward' on the front cover of *Men's Health* or why transformation is an important idea in a make-up advert such as *That Boss Life part 1*, is more complex. Your understanding will develop the more you engage with the media theories and ideas and the more you apply them to the CSPs.

Revision activities will be offered in all chapters and you will find some specific examination tips throughout the book. Activities can be adapted to deal with different ideas and CSPs as you find the revision techniques that work best for you. Everyone thinks and works differently, so it is important to find the activities that will help you gain the knowledge you need and then apply the knowledge to help you develop your understanding.

For specific exam technique advice see Chapter 9, pages 183–200 of the Year 1 & AS student book.

As with most things, the best way to become good at something is to practise. You can practise using the terms and ideas from the media framework every time you read, watch, listen to, play or access any media product. For example, you could:

- Practise identifying media language choices and persuasive techniques when you see adverts on billboards while you are on a bus.
- Practise considering the way the representations of people, places or ideas are constructed in the magazine you flick through while waiting for a hair-cut.
- Practise identifying the many ways you access advertising and marketing in your day-to-day life and look for they way audiences are defined and targeted, and the way persuasive techniques are used.
- Practise looking for narrative roles and the structure of the story when watching a film or a series on Netflix or another streaming service.

The media is part of most people's day-to-day activity and Media Studies shouldn't just be a subject that is studied for an examination. Media Studies should inform the way you select and interpret the media that surrounds you.

You can still enjoy all sorts of media from the fun and frothy to the more serious, but, once you have studied the subject in detail, you will understand the way the media works to gain and keep your attention and the way it tries to create meaning. Becoming a good Media Studies student is something you can work on every day and this will make answering the questions in the examination feel more like simply telling the examiner what you think rather than an exercise in memory.

The chapters in this revision guide will include the following:

- **Spec Spotlight:** a reminder about the examiner's expectations from the exam board specification. These will often include essential terms you will need to learn for the examination.
- **Examples** of analysis and the application of theoretical ideas.
- **Revision Booster:** ideas and suggestions to help you revise more effectively.

- **Tip:** a tip to help you when you are in the exam room.
- **Links** to the student books that you can refer to in order to help you extend your knowledge and understanding.

Some important terms

- **Media forms:** the different types of media largely based on the way information is presented to the audience. For example, television is a media form.
- **Media products:** specific examples of the media within each of the forms. For example, *Loose Women* and *Bodyguard* are both television products.
- **Close study products (CSPs):** the named products identified by the exam board that must be referred to in the exam.
- **Non-exam assessment (NEA):** the practical production-based assessment task based on briefs published by the exam board.

Chapter 1 Media language

SPEC SPOTLIGHT

This is from the AQA specification:

In this section students will develop their knowledge and understanding of:
- how the different modes and language associated with different media forms communicate
- multiple meanings
- how the combination of elements of media language influence meaning
- how developing technologies affect media language
- the codes and conventions of media forms and products, including the processes through which media language develops as genre
- the dynamic and historically relative nature of genre
- the processes through which meanings are established through intertextuality
- how audiences respond to and interpret the above aspects of media language.

Introduction

The study of media language is central to Media Studies. Put simply, Media Studies is the study of the relationships between media producers and audiences, and it is media products that create these relationships. Media producers use media language to create media products, and audiences use their understanding of media language to interpret and understand the messages being communicated.

> **REVISION BOOSTER**
>
> **Media language has been divided into three sections to help with revision:**
> 1 Making meaning
> 2 Genre
> 3 Narrative

1.1 Making meaning

Media students need to understand how media language is chosen to create messages and how media language is 'read' by audiences. This means that there are two sides to the study of this area of the theoretical framework and in preparation for the exams you will need to revise the terms and ideas related to both:

a The specifics of media language choices made in the construction of media products.

b The terms and ideas used to discuss the way media language creates meaning.

The construction of media products

Platform, form and genre

Media products are made up of images, words and sounds. How they are put together depends on the platform used to distribute the product. Different **forms** use media language differently and you should be aware of the way the **platform** and the **form** set up a template for production.

The platform used to distribute a media product sets up a **paradigm** for production based on practical limitations, and the forms within each platform are based around the

A Star is Born website

function of each media product, its content and/or the requirements of the audience.

ACTIVITY 1.1

1   Add to the examples of forms common in each platform.

2   Name some specific examples of each form – use examples from your own knowledge as well as from the CSPs you have studied.

Media platform	Media language used	Examples of form	Specific media products
Print	Uses text and images only.	Newspapers	The *Daily Mail*, the *i*
Broadcast (audio)	Audio products use music, sound effects and the spoken word to communicate to audiences.	Music radio	
Broadcast (video)	Video products use images as well as sound. Video can use the spoken word as well as words on screen as required.	News bulletin	
e-Media	Can use still and moving imagery; can use audio consisting of sound, music and/or the spoken word; can use words in both short and long form.	Advertising website	

You need to be familiar with the restrictions of each platform and the general codes and conventions of the forms. You also need to be familiar with the different ways media language is selected and used in the different forms. You do not need to memorise definitions for these terms but you should be familiar with what they mean and how they can be used to create meaning.

Moving image:

- cinematography
- sound
- mise-en-scène
- editing
- special effects.

Different worlds in *The Hunger Games* are conveyed by Effie Trinket from the Capitol (left) and Katniss from District 12 (right).

Audio:

- dialogue
- sound effects
- foley
- ambient sound
- music
- jingles
- idents.

Print:

- lexis
- register
- tone
- style
- pace.

Images:

- mise-en-scène
- angle
- camera position
- framing
- cropping
- in-camera effects
- post-production effects.

Sound mixing desk

The front covers of these magazines generate expectations about the contents.

Point-of-view shot

ACTIVITY 1.2

1 Look at these images. What camera shots are being used?

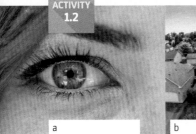

a

b

c

d

2 Look at this example of a magazine front cover. Identify the media language choices as marked.

Image Alexi Lubomirski / GQ
© The Condé Naste Publications Ltd

The terms and ideas you learn in your study of media language will be used across both sections of the examination paper regardless of which areas of the framework you are being assessed on.

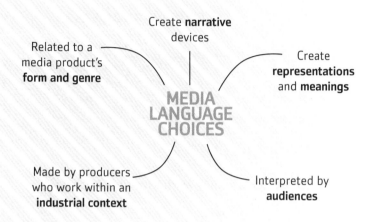

MEDIA LANGUAGE CHOICES

Create **narrative** devices

Related to a media product's **form and genre**

Create **representations** and **meanings**

Made by producers who work within an **industrial context**

Interpreted by **audiences**

Media language choices are used to create meaning and when you discuss the other areas of the framework you should use specific examples from your CSPs to support the point you want to make.

TIP

Using specific examples means offering details from the media product you are discussing. For example, you could say that *Men's Health* magazine uses its cover to attract the target audience. That is correct but is very vague. Saying that it uses a celebrity to attract the target audience is better but still not specific to the CSP. Saying that the film actor Vin Diesel is presented on the front cover of *Men's Health* in an attempt to attract and appeal to the target audience is a detailed and specific example.

Before the exam, practise using specific and detailed examples from each CSP to support your thoughts and ideas about the product.

Knowledge

Following are the terms and ideas you **need** to know. You should know what each of these **essential terms/ideas** means in preparation for the examination.

You should practise writing definitions for the terms, as you could be asked to do so in the exam. Alternatively, you could be given a definition and be asked to identify the term being referred to, so you must know what all these terms mean.

ESSENTIAL MEDIA LANGUAGE TERMS AND IDEAS

Semiotics:
- sign
- signifier
- signified
- dominant signifier
- icon
- index
- code
- symbol
- anchorage
- ideology
- paradigm
- syntagm.

Barthes' ideas and theories on semiotics:
- signification
- denotation
- connotation
- myth.

ACTIVITY 1.3

1 Here are some definitions of terms on the list above. Identify which term is being defined.

Definition	Term
The meaning or idea communicated by the use of a specific sign.	
The image or sound used to communicate an idea.	
An image or sound that is known to represent a specific object or idea but is not a literal representation of it.	

2 Write a definition for each of the following terms:

a index

b ideology

c myth

d dominant signifier

e anchorage.

3 Explain the difference between:

a paradigm and syntagm

b denotation and connotation.

Application

You apply theory by using the terms from the theoretical framework to discuss the way a media product is communicating meaning to the audience.

Chapters 1, 2 and 3 of the Year 1 & AS student book provide more details and examples covering the application of the media language area of the theoretical framework. Each chapter focuses on different media platforms and forms.

EXAMPLE

The media product shown on the right is using media language choices that commonly **connote** wealth, luxury and success. The sleek and shiny car is positioned in the foreground immediately in front of a **symbol** of power and wealth – a yacht. A second yacht can be seen on the left and the backdrop to the image is a city skyline with skyscrapers that are also **symbols** of wealth, business and success. The idea of the gleaming car

is **anchored** in the lexis with the use of the word 'reflected', creating an association between the car and success, and the car reflects the 'world' of its owner: a world of luxury and success. These ideas are part of the **cultural myth** that success is measured by the ability to buy certain types of products, in this case a car. The advert reflects the **ideologies** of materialism, where success and status is measured by what a person buys.

A hegemonic reading (Hall)

The producer of the advert wants the audience to associate the product being advertised with status. The **encoded intended meaning** of the advert is that buying this product would give the purchaser a social status by communicating their economic success to others. The advert wants the reader to see the product as something that is desirable and will act as a symbol of the driver's status. Readers **decode** a **preferred reading** when they see the product, accept it as a symbol of success and status, and desire to own it based on these ideas.

A negotiated reading (Hall)

The reader could understand the message and partially accept it. Here, perhaps, the product would be associated with luxury, success and status but the audience members may reject the need to demonstrate their own status with a car when they **decode** the message.

An oppositional reading (Hall)

Readers could see the message being **encoded** but rather than see the car as a status symbol they might criticise the materialistic values communicated by the advert, preferring to value people by what they do rather than what they own.

REVISION BOOSTER

You can practise analysing media products by breaking down the media language choices made at any time. Try to get in the habit of using your knowledge and understanding whenever you encounter a media product.

ACTIVITY 1.4 Repeat the thought process shown, using the Jaguar car advert on page 15, by answering the following questions referring to the still below from a Breitling watch campaign featuring David Beckham.

1 Encoding: list the media language choices that have been used in this advert that connote wealth, luxury and success.

2 Encoding: identify the producer's intended meaning – what would be the preferred reading of this advert?

3 Decoding: identify how someone may make a negotiated reading of the advertising image.

4 Decoding: make an oppositional reading of the advertising image.

1.2 Genre

Introduction

Media products are often grouped into categories by their 'shared characteristics'. The shared characteristic could be based on:

- the style or look of the product (the way Westerns share a similar look)
- the content of the product (the way all lifestyle magazines provide similar content)
- the emotional effect created by the product (the way all horrors aim to scare the audience)
- the type of story told (the way all soap operas focus on domestic stories).

 TIP Ideas about genre are assessed as part of the media language area of the theoretical framework.

Physical audience responses

REVISION BOOSTER

Recognising a genre is the first step but in the study of genre you will need to engage with:

1 how genre is a **model for production** – creating templates and also restricting production choices

2 how genre creates meanings for the **audience** and the importance of audience expectations

3 how genres have to **change and adapt** to maintain audience interest

4 how genre can be a way to **tell a story**.

ESSENTIAL MEDIA LANGUAGE TERMS AND IDEAS

Genre conventions and rules:

- sub-genre
- hybridity
- genres of order and integration
- 'genre as cultural category'.

Genre and production

Genre is a way to categorise media products by grouping them together via their shared characteristics. These characteristics are called the **codes** and **conventions**. This means that within a specific form (e.g. newspapers) there can be several genres. They all use the codes and conventions of newspaper design but also present information in a way that is specific to each type (genre) of newspaper.

The need to use genre codes and conventions means that media producers are not free to use any media language choices they wish. The form of media product limits the choices (e.g. there is no way to use sound in a print production) and the genre of each media products also limits the choices that are available.

All newspapers share the same codes and conventions of the form. Newspapers are printed on paper and each page is divided into columns Headlines are used to summarise a story's content, and images are used as illustrations. Most newspapers present stories in short paragraphs with sub-headings indicating key aspects of the story, and pictures will be presented with captions to help explain what is being shown.

However, not all newspapers are the same. In the UK we tend to think of our newspapers as belonging to one of three distinct genres:

- broadsheet   • mid-market tabloid   • tabloid (red-tops).

Each genre has its own codes and conventions in the visual presentation of the newspaper, in the type of stories it selects and in its approach to the content of the stories.

Different ways to report on the birth of a royal prince.

Identify the codes and conventions of each genre of British newspaper.

	Broadsheets	Mid-market tabloids	Tabloids
	The *Daily Telegraph*; the *Daily Guardian*; the *i*	The *Daily Express*; the *Daily Mail*	The *Daily Mirror*; the *Sun*
Appearance (layout and design)			Images dominate over words
News values (content)			Value soft news over hard news; often report on gossip, scandal and human interest stories
Reporting style (lexis and tone)			Informal tone; simple lexis; often use puns and sensationalism
General approach to newsworthy events	Often take a 'global' or big picture approach. How does the event impact on society/culture/the political landscape?	Often take a localised approach. How does the event impact on my life or the lives of my family?	Often take a personalised approach: how does this impact on me (or people like me)?

Genre creates restrictions, but it also creates templates for media producers to follow.

Imagine you are a sub-editor for a newspaper. Your job is to write a headline for a story about a speech the Prime Minister gave saying the government planned to raise taxes for people with large salaries.

Considering the conventions of each genre of newspaper, create a headline for each. Consider how you will refer to the Prime Minister and how you will present the idea of raised taxes for the wealthy.

1 Broadsheet headline:

2 Mid-market tabloid headline:

3 Tabloid headline:

Genre helps media producers, as the infinite possibility of **media language** choices is reduced by the codes and conventions of the genre.

ACTIVITY 1.7

Sit-coms and crime dramas are genres of television programme. How do the **paradigms** of each genre limit the choices available to media producers? Identify some of the ways conventional examples of these two genres will use media language differently.

Media language	Sit-com	Crime drama
Use of camera		
Use of sound	Canned laughter/studio audience; upbeat music	Atmospheric music; use of silence to create unease
Use of lighting		
Types of plot		
Types of character		

Genre and audience

Genre not only helps media producers, it also helps audiences know what to expect from a media product. Audiences can 'frame their expectations' when they know what a genre is likely to provide. When sitting down to watch a sit-com, the audience will expect light, humorous entertainment and, hopefully, the programme will make them laugh. When sitting down to watch a crime drama, the audience will expect to be kept in suspense and to feel tense while watching the programme. Audiences use genre to select (and reject) media products because the basic 'rules' for each genre are known by both producers and the audience.

ACTIVITY 1.8

1 You can read just one type of magazine. Would it be:
   - a health and fitness magazine ☐
   - a fashion magazine ☐
   - a DIY magazine ☐
   - a cookery magazine? ☐

2 You can watch only one type of film. Would it be:
   - a superhero film ☐
   - a comedy ☐
   - a horror ☐
   - a thriller? ☐

3 Are there any genres of any media forms you would actively avoid?

Genre development

Comedies that are not funny, or horrors that are not frightening, have failed as the basic expectations of the audience aren't met and so the audience is disappointed. Audience expectations change over time and if a genre keeps offering its audiences the same thing, audiences can become bored. **Neale** says that 'genres rely on repetition and difference'. Genres that simply repeat themselves are doomed to fail with audiences eventually; whereas genres that adapt and change, while staying true to some fundamental genre conventions, are more likely to remain popular with audiences.

ACTIVITY 1.9

How would creating a **hybrid** media product help avoid audiences becoming bored with a genre?

Genre as a way to tell a story

Interstellar (2014) uses codes and conventions of sci-fi.

The most common way to identify a genre is through the iconographic **codes and conventions** – the visual (and sometimes audio) indicators of a genre.

Although there are many different types of sci-fi, some of the common iconographic codes and conventions in the genre are:

- use of futuristic technology
- futuristic architecture/décor
- robots/artificial intelligence (AI) machines
- use of futuristic weapons
- futuristic clothing
- lots of silver and blue in the mise-en-scène
- computerised sound effects.

In addition, there are certain types of stories common in the genre, for example stories about space exploration or plots based on the impact of technology.

ACTIVITY 1.10

What are some of the common codes and conventions for the Western genre? What would you expect to see and hear in examples of this genre?

Visual and audio codes and conventions help us to recognise a genre and place other similar products in the same category. These codes and conventions also help us recognise genre **hybridity**.

Westworld is a television product that is a **hybrid** of Western and sci-fi genre conventions. The Western had been the most successful genre in the middle of the 20th century but has struggled to find a modern audience. Occasional, more recent, Western films have been successful but, in the main, the Western hasn't been able to adapt to contemporary audience needs. Its stories about masculine heroes, disputes over land ownership and the demonisation of Native Americans don't fit in with modern interests and values, so the genre has fallen out of favour.

Sci-fi, however, has remained a successful genre, with many different types of sci-fi appealing to many different audiences. *Westworld* bought together the codes and conventions of both genres, creating a television series that was popular with critics and audiences.

Westworld used codes and conventions of sci-fi and Westerns.

The Western elements of *Westworld* gave the audience the escapism of a violent, lawless past but the story was framed as being within a futuristic theme park, so referenced gaming, cos-play culture and virtual reality entertainment. The sci-fi elements created the 'what if?' fantasy of a future world and this became the setting for a thriller narrative. The combination of the two genres provided a range of gratifications for the audience and the hybrid nature of the product helped to provide the 'familiarity' (Neale) that allowed the audience to create expectations of characters and plot development as well as the 'difference' that offered new experiences and allowed them to be surprised by the development of the story.

Visual codes and conventions are based on the surface appearance of a media product, so only really help us describe a genre. Within each genre different products communicate many different meanings. One way to consider the meaning created by products within a genre is to use the idea of 'genres of order and integration'. This allows us to analyse a media product while considering the way its narrative structure creates meaning.

ACTIVITY 1.11

1 Using your television CSP, identify how it fits in with Schatz's ideas about the **genre of order and/or integration**.

Genres of order	TV CSP	Genres of integration	TV CSP
The hero tends to be a lone individual – traditionally, the hero would be male.		**The hero** is often a collective, a family, a couple or community. Female or feminine heroes may feature.	
The setting is a contested space – a location that is being argued or fought over. The setting is ideologically unstable.		**The setting** is a civilised space that is largely ideologically stable. Settings are often communities or families.	
The conflict is often based on an externalised threat and is usually expressed through violence.		**The conflict** is internalised – the threat to the community comes from conflict between the members of the group and is expressed through emotion.	
The resolution will usually mean the elimination of the conflict, often via a literal or symbolic death.		**The resolution** will usually be in the form of an embrace, love or some form of unification.	
Common themes include the hero taking on the problems and contradictions of the world they inhabit on behalf of others – protecting and saving those weaker than them. A 'macho' code of behaviour dominates. The hero is often isolated and self-reliant The hero often doesn't benefit from the resolution – they may leave after saving the community or may die in the act of resolving the conflict. The hero is an individual who remains outside the community.		**Common themes** include those involved in the conflict becoming integrated into the wider community once their personal problems have been resolved. There is a maternal/familial code of behaviour that dominates the story. The resolution often shows the value of community, communication and cooperation.	

2 Is your TV CSP part of the genre of order or the genre of integration, or is it a hybrid of the two?

The genres of order and integration help us move beyond the look or the sound of a genre and help us consider the way the story creates meaning. A crime drama that shows how a crime can only be solved by a collection of people working together, or how a family or community have to work together to survive after a tragedy, is very different in tone from one where a lone-wolf detective is the only person who can save the community from an external threat. These two approaches to the genre communicate different values and attitudes and so create different types of gratifications. This is one way that genre can be seen to be a **cultural category** rather than one that is just based on the look or content of a media product.

ACTIVITY 1.12

You can apply this theory to non-fiction media products such as newspapers, where the 'stories' they tell are sometimes less obvious.

Apply the above ideas to the following CSPs.

	Genre of order/integration
Men's Health	The reader is challenged to fight the externalised conflicts (Christmas food, alcohol) that stops him from having the perfect male physique. The magazine will help him by setting goals, offering advice and providing images of his objective (Vin Diesel's body) but the reader must act alone. Exercise can be used to violently destroy the conflicts standing in his way.
TeenVogue.com	
The _i_	
Tomb Raider: Anniversary	

This theory focuses on the idea of the hero and how the hero deals with conflict. As you will see, these are two important ideas that are part of the study of narrative: the third aspect of media language that you need to know and understand for the examination.

1.3 Narrative

Introduction

Media language choices construct narrative devices that help structure the story being told. Stories consist of events (the **plot**) and these events need to be organised and arranged for audiences to understand what is happening – this organisation is the **narrative structure**.

There are some key ideas about narrative that you will need to know for the examination. These are ideas are identified in the AQA specification.

ESSENTIAL MEDIA LANGUAGE TERMS AND IDEAS

Narratology:

- narrative codes
- narration
- diegesis
- quest narrative
- 'character types'
- causality
- plot
- masterplot.

Todorov's ideas and theories on narratology:

- equilibrium
- disruption
- new equilibrium.

REVISION **BOOSTER**

To help with revision, try to think about narrative in the following ways:

1 As a **structure** that takes the audience from the beginning of the story to its end and, in doing this, how narrative codes are used to provide information.

2 As a structure that uses **characters** who have a role in the development of events.

3 As a structure centred around the use of **binary oppositions** – this is related to the different types of stories that are told (**masterplots**).

Narrative structure

A basic story has **a beginning, a middle and an end**. Narrative theory shows that in conventional narratives these three parts of the story tend to follow the same type of conventions – even though stories, settings, characters and events may vary.

EXAMPLE

The Killing is a 20-episode series with the major **narrative disruption** occurring at the very start of Episode 1 with the murder of Nanna Birk Larsen. The protagonist, Sarah Lund, is introduced just as her life is about to move into a new **equilibrium**. At the start of the episode she is preparing to move house and leave her job to marry her fiancé. The murder of Nanna becomes a **disruptive event** in Lund's life because she begins to prioritise her work over her private life, continuing to investigate the murder and postponing travelling to meet her fiancé.

BAFTA WINNER
BEST INTERNATIONAL AWARD

"Classy, compelling television"
DAILY TELEGRAPH

"The new THE WIRE"
SUNDAY TIMES

"Seductively good"
THE INDEPENDENT

THE KILLING

When the audience are introduced to the Larsen family, the mother and father are unaware of Nanna's death and so appear to be in a state of **equilibrium**. The **disruptions** to their domestic life are provided when Nanna has been identified and her family are informed about her death. The following episodes show the **progress** of the investigation and the family's response to the loss. Further **problems** in the investigation are experienced until, in the final episode, the **mystery** is solved and the characters find themselves in their **new equilibrium**.

ACTIVITY 1.13

1 Using your television CSP, identify how these ideas can be evidenced in the first episode, by completing the following table.

	The Missing	*The Killing*	*Deutschland 83*
Equilibrium		Sarah is to be married and is moving house. Pernille and Theis are happily married.	
Disequilibrium		The episode begins with the attack on Nanna.	Martin is recruited to work undercover and is relocated to West Germany.
New equilibrium		By the end of the episode, Sarah is established as the lead investigator and is putting her private life on hold.	Martin is working as a spy.

2 If you have watched the whole series, identify how this structure can be evidenced across the whole series.

	The Missing	*The Killing*	*Deutschland 83*
Equilibrium			
Disequilibrium			
New equilibrium			

Character types

Every story is populated with characters. These characters will be very different – some will be quiet and thoughtful, others more extrovert. Some will have positive character traits and others will be selfish or even pure evil. However, Propp identified that, regardless of the genre or type of story being told, all stories use a number of set characters that can be defined by their **function** in terms of the way they **move the world of the story** towards its **new equilibrium**.

ACTIVITY 1.14

Propp identified lots of characters that turn up time and time again in stories. Define the following roles by their function in the narrative. Give an example of this type of character in your television CSP. Bear in mind that characters in stories play different roles at different points in the narrative, so one character may have several roles. Also, damsels and princesses are not always females.

Character role	Function in the narrative	Example from TV CSP
Helper	Aids the hero/protagonist in achieving their goal, solving the problems, sorting out conflicts and moving the world through the disruption into a new equilibrium.	
Dispatcher		
Damsel in distress		
Hero/protagonist		
Villain/antagonist	Stands in the way of the hero/protagonist and attempts to stop them achieving their goals.	
Princess		

Binary opposites

As you have seen, narratives need to progress and the main way this is achieved is in the use of binary oppositions. Most narratives are based on some form of opposition whether it is:

- Knowledge vs Mystery as in *The Missing*
- The Criminal vs Police as in *The Killing*
- East (communism) vs West (capitalism) as in *Deutschland 83*.

Binary oppositions set up **conflicts** that become the **disruptive events** of the story. Without these conflicts, there is no story.

For example: *The Killing*:

- A girl is murdered (the disruptive event).
- Sarah Lund attempts to find out who did it – the conflicts are between:
  - the police and the criminal
  - lies vs the truth
  - the mystery and the solution
  - criminal actions vs the rule of law
  - crime vs justice.

Sarah's desires conflict with the desires of the criminal:

- Sarah wants to solve the crime – the criminal wants to get away with the crime.
- Sarah wants to re-establish the rule of law – the criminal wishes to avoid capture and punishment.

The basic conflict between Sarah's desire to solve the case and the criminal's desire to avoid detection influence the decisions made and the actions taken, so these conflicts allow the story to develop and move forwards.

Finally, narratives not only use specific character roles to tell their stories, they also often use masterplots.

The narrative of television and radio dramas should be easy to identify, as telling the story in an interesting and engaging way is one of the functions of the form. As the story takes place over a period of time, the narrative can be seen to move and progress. Less straightforward, however, is the way masterplots are used in other types of media product.

1 In the table below some masterplots are listed. Write a brief description of the events you would expect in each masterplot and suggest two or three media products that use this masterplot.

2 Can you identify masterplots that are used by any of your CSPs?

Masterplot	Description	For example	CSP
Quest narrative	A story based on a journey based on a search for a person, place or thing.		*The Missing*: based on the search for the truth about what happened to a missing child.
Revenge narrative			
Transformation narrative			*Men's Health*: the magazine helps the reader transform his body.
Discovery narrative			
Maturation narrative	The 'coming of age story' – usually based around an event that takes the protagonist from being a child to becoming a young adult.		
Escape narrative			
Underdog narrative	A story based on someone fighting against adversity or some form of oppression.		*Hidden Figures*: shows how some black women battled racism and sexism to become successful in their profession.

SUMMARY

Media language

- Media products are constructed using a combination of elements depending on the product's form and genre.
- These elements are carefully chosen to combine to **create meaning**.
- Media language combines to create **genre codes**.
- Media language combines to create **narrative devices**.
- Media language is used to **communicate ideas to the audience who then interpret the messages** in media products.

> **TIP** Practise applying these narrative ideas to your CSPs, as you could be asked a specific question about the way your CSPs use narrative structures and roles to tell their stories.

Chapter 2 Media representations

SPEC SPOTLIGHT

This is from the AQA specification:

In this section students will develop their knowledge and understanding of:

- the way events, issues, individuals (including self-representation) and social groups (including social identity) are represented through processes of selection and combination
- the way the media construct versions of reality through re-presentation
- the processes which lead media producers to make choices about how to represent events, issues, individuals and social groups
- the effect of social and cultural context on representations
- how and why stereotypes can be used positively and negatively
- how and why particular social groups, in a national and global context, may be underrepresented or misrepresented
- how media representations convey values, attitudes and beliefs about the world and how these may be systematically reinforced across a wide range of media representations
- how audiences respond to and interpret media representations.

⌕ Further details, definitions and explanations of media representation terms and ideas can be found in the Year 1 & AS Media Studies student book in Chapter 4.

Introduction

When media language elements are combined to create a media product, representations are created. Representations are the re-presentation of ideas, places, people, groups and things in media products. However realistic the media product appears, no representations can ever be 'real' as they are the product of decisions made by directors, designers, photographers, editors and writers. Representations, therefore, create a **constructed reality**.

> **REVISION BOOSTER**
>
> As we have learned when studying media language, media products all have an intended meaning, and representations are used to try and communicate ideas to the audience. You need to understand how representations are constructed using media language. You will also need to be able to show your **knowledge** of the terms and ideas related to representation and your **understanding** of how representation works by applying these ideas to media products.
>
> You should practise using these ideas when engaging with media products day to day.

Following are the terms and ideas you **need** to know. You should know what each of these **essential terms/ideas** means in preparation for the examination.

ESSENTIAL REPRESENTATION TERMS AND IDEAS

Theories of representation:
- positive and negative stereotypes
- countertypes
- misrepresentation
- selective representation
- dominant ideology
- constructed reality
- hegemony
- audience positioning.

Hall's ideas and theories on representation:
- encoding/decoding (see Activity 2.4 and Section 2.2 of this chapter).

Theories of identity as summarised by Gauntlett:
- fluidity of identity
- constructed identity
- negotiated identity
- collective identity.

The starting point for your revision will need to be **remembering** these terms and what they mean. You will not be able to progress to a more in-depth **understanding** until you have learned the definitions.

ACTIVITY 2.1

1 Make flashcards that define the essential terms and ideas (on page 30).

2 Using your mobile phone, create a short video in the style of a simple, single camera YouTube vlog and record a definition of each term from your flashcards. You can then re-watch the video to help you memorise the definitions.

TIP In the exam you could be asked to write definitions of terms, select the correct definitions or identify representation ideas in media products.

REVISION BOOSTER

You may find it helpful to use the following categories to help revise representation:

1 The construction of meaning
2 The use of stereotypes
3 Problems with representations
4 Representations and identity

2.1 The construction of meaning

The combining of media language elements can be used to create **positive** and **negative** representations, and media producers try to control the messages that they communicate when they create media products. These ideas are **encoded** by the media producers in ways that try to ensure the audience **decode** the intended meaning.

ACTIVITY 2.2

1 Imagine you need to create the following ideas when creating a representation. What media language elements could you use to **encode** your message?

You are making a video news report about your home town. How would you create a positive representation using media language? Consider **what** you would show and **how** you would show it.	
You are writing a film review for your blog-site. The film is called *Superheroes to the Rescue*. You didn't like the film. Create a headline that would represent the film negatively.	
You are directing a television drama and you want to show that your policeman protagonist is 'a man of mystery' with deep and possibly dark secrets. What media language choices would you make to create this representation? Also consider costume, location, props, lighting, camera work, acting direction, etc.	
You need to select a picture of the Prime Minister that is going on the front page of the tabloid newspaper you edit, to accompany a story about a decision to create a new national bank holiday. The front page will be limited to the picture of the Prime Minister and a brief (but large) headline. Your newspaper supports the government's decision. Describe the type of image you would use and write a headline to represent the decision positively.	

(Continued)

2 Now repeat the exercise changing the **encoded** meaning of the representations you are creating.

You are making a video news report about your home town. How would you create a negative representation using media language? Consider **what** you would show and **how** you would show it.	
You are writing a film review for your blog-site. The film is called *Superheroes to the Rescue*. You loved the film. Create a headline that would represent the film positively.	
You are directing a television drama and you want to show that your policeman protagonist is a happy and upbeat person. What media language choices would you make to create this representation? Also consider costume, location, props, lighting, camera work, acting direction, etc.	
You need to select a picture of the Prime Minister that is going on the front page of the tabloid newspaper you edit, to accompany a story about a decision to create a new national bank holiday. The front page will be limited to the picture of the Prime Minister and a brief (but large) headline. Your newspaper does not support the government's decision. Describe the type of image you would use and write a headline to represent the decision negatively.	

By selecting media language elements to communicate a specific idea you are **positioning the audience** to decode a specific meaning.

ACTIVITY 2.3

How do these front pages use their headlines to **position their audience**? What meanings are the audience expected to decode from the media language choices? What emotional response are they expected to have?

The day after the Brexit referendum 2016

Ideas can be communicated when there is a **cultural agreement** in the meaning of specific media language choices. Some items of clothing bring meaning to the person wearing them because of the connotations they create. The meaning of these connotations is understood by most people within the culture.

ACTIVITY
2.4 Consider how you would communicate the following ideas visually so that the meaning was **encoded** in a single image? Choose from the media language choices on the right of the following table to create the meanings offered on the left, then draw your representation in the middle column.

The male character in a Western is heroic.		
The female in a soap opera is the life and soul of the party.		• Reading glasses and a roll-neck jumper • A hoody and baseball cap • A white hat • Oversized jewellery and bright clothing
The female detective is an introvert.		
The young male in the drama cannot be trusted.		

The wardrobe choices on the right of the table have no meaning in themselves but we share a cultural agreement that they represent certain personality traits and contribute to stereotypes about certain types of people. Media products rely on **stereotypes** to communicate ideas to the audience. **Stereotypes** can communicate complex ideas quickly and efficiently but can also lead to oversimplifications about groups of people.

2.2 The use of stereotypes

ACTIVITY 2.5

1 List some of the groups and types of people represented in any of your CSPs. What **stereotypes** about this group are represented in the product?

CSP	Stereotypes
The Killing	Theiss is a stereotypical grieving father, as he is shown responding with anger and violence. Pernille is a stereotypical grieving mother, as she is shown expressing her emotions by crying and physical distress. Sarah is a stereotypical detective who has personal issues to deal with that she ignores/supresses while she stays focused on her work, and seems to prioritise her duty to strangers over that of her responsibilities to her family.
The Missing	
Deutschland 83	
Men's Health	
That Boss Life part 1	
Tomb Raider: Anniversary	

2 Develop your understanding of stereotypes by considering these questions:

a Which, if any, of the stereotypes identified above do you think are positive and which are negative?

b Do you think that positive stereotypes can be problematic?

c What negative effects might stereotypes create?

All stereotypes are **selective**. They show limited aspects of the subject of representation. Stereotypes may be based on ideas that can be true. For example, some men do respond violently to grief as Theiss does in *The Killing*, but not all men do. Stereotypes can create narrow ideas and misrepresent the group by implying that they are all the same. This happens when places are represented based on very select and limited ideas of the place such as 'London is glamorous and filled with wealthy people'. That's partially true but the stereotypes hide the fact that many low-paid people and homeless people live there. Stereotypes often feed into the **dominant ideologies** held by the culture about groups, places, ideas and things reflecting the **hegemonic** ideals shared by the producing culture.

 ACTIVITY 2.6

What **dominate ideologies** and **hegemonic ideals** are supported by the following stereotypes?

a Grieving men often respond aggressively.

b London is a glamorous and wealthy city.

c Detectives are bad at personal relationships.

d Men show their strength by looking muscly and having short hair.

e Most men in US prisons are black.

2.3 Problems with representations

Misrepresentations create false ideas about the people, places or things being represented. Some media producers create **countertypes** to try to correct the commonly held ideas created by selective representations or misrepresentations. All representations, whether they are positive or negative, stereotypes or countertypes, create a constructed reality, as no representation can ever be truly accurate or complete.

 ACTIVITY 2.7

Identify how stereotypes about American black men are being challenged in the video for 'Letter to the Free':

1 What are the **stereotypes** being challenged?

2 What **countertypes** are created in the music video?

3 How does the video create a **constructed reality** about black men's experiences in the US today?

2.4 Representations and identity

Representations of people, either individuals or groups, can create ideas about the **identity** of these people.

Which of your CSPs create representations of the following?

a Gender identity (masculine and/or feminine identity)?

b Sexual identity (LGBTQ and/or straight identity)?

c Racial identity (e.g. Caucasian, African-American, British Asian)?

d Religious identity (e.g. Hindu, Muslim, Christian)?

e Others?

The media participate in the construction of identities. They often repeat traditional ideas about what these groups are like. These **hegemonic ideas** about identity are traditionally easy to define and seen as fixed.

1 Select the terms from the list below that best define the qualities of **hegemonic masculinity**. Name the traditional qualities that define what it is to be masculine. Add other terms to your list.

2 Select the terms from the list below that best define the qualities of **hegemonic femininity**. Name the traditional qualities that define what it is to be feminine. Add other terms to your list.

Tip: hegemonic femininity is usually the binary opposite of hegemonic masculinity.

strong   loud   emotional   weak   unemotional   small   quiet   large   passive
aggressive   logical   intuitive   worker   nurturer   provider   domestic   active   still

Masculine traits	Feminine traits

Gemma Webster in *The Missing*

To be outside the hegemonic ideals of gender used is to be seen as being wrong or in some way 'not normal'. Hegemonic ideals are often represented positively, and subversions of the ideals negatively.

1 Identify how representations in *Men's Health* relate to hegemonic masculinity. Are the audience positioned to find these ideas positive or negative?

2 Identify how Sarah or Pernille in *The Killing*, Gemma in *The Missing* or Maria in *Deutschland 83* reinforce or subvert ideas about hegemonic femininity. Are the audience positioned to respond to the character positively or negatively?

Masculine women and feminine men are still often treated with suspicion or seen negatively. Feminine men are often presented as being 'incomplete' or 'less than' in some way, whereas 'masculine' women are often shown as abrasive and qualities such as being ambitious are seen as character flaws rather than positive traits, as they usually are for men. However, many representations show identity as being **fluid** rather than firm or fixed.

ACTIVITY 2.11

1 Is Manny Guttierez (right) represented as having a masculine, feminine or fluid gender identity in the Maybelline *That Boss Life part 1* advert?

2 Support your observations by identifying how he is represented in the Maybelline advert.

Representations traditionally considered masculine	Representations traditionally considered feminine

3 Does the advert position the audience to see Manny's gender identity in a positive or negative way?

Audiences can use media products to help them construct an idea of their own identity. Fluid identity means that traits can be selected and rejected from multiple sources, so audiences can define themselves in lots of different and changeable ways. As you have seen, gender identity is constructed differently in *Men's Health* and *That Boss Life part 1*, and both offer audiences the ability for audiences to **negotiate** their own gender identity as individuals and as members of a larger group.

We all have our own identities, but we also identify with a number of different groups.

1 List the different types of groups you identify with.

You might start by identifying groups based on your age, race, religion, gender, job, religion, nationality, region, county or town you live in, sexuality, political point-of-view, sporting interests, hobbies, celebrity interests or musical tastes. Some of the groups you are in may not be ones you've chosen such as your biological sex or ethnicity, but you might be an active member of some groups or just an interested observer on the edges of others.

Groups I identify with:

2 Now list media products that represent ideas about any of these groups.

3 Do you think the representations are always fair and accurate?

4 Do you think the representations are always unfair and inaccurate?

5 Do you think the representations have elements of truth in them at times?

If you agree with question 3 in Activity 2.12, you are **negotiating** the definition of your identity by **selecting** and **rejecting** some of the ideas presented in the media.

When we are members of groups we can negotiate our own identities but most **collective identities** have key ideas that connect members of the groups together.

SUMMARY

Representation

- Representations are **re-presentations of people, places, ideas and things.**
- Media language is **selected and combined** to make representations.
- Selection is used to communicate specific ideas about the subject of the representation.
- Media producers construct representations to reflect certain **ideas and values**.
- **Audiences interpret** these representations.
- **Stereotypes** are often used as they communicate ideas quickly and can be recognised by the audience as they are used across a variety of media.
- Traditionally, representations are created by the culture's most powerful groups and reflect their world-view.
- Media representations can be used to communicate ideas about **identities**.
- **Media audiences** may use the media to help understand their own and other people's identities.

Chapter 3

Media audiences and industries

SPEC SPOTLIGHT

This is from the AQA specification:

In this section students will develop their knowledge and understanding of:

- how audiences are grouped and categorised by media industries, including by age, gender and social class, as well as by lifestyle and taste
- how media producers target, attract, reach, address and potentially construct audiences
- how media industries target audiences through the content and appeal of media products and through the ways in which they are marketed, distributed and circulated
- the interrelationship between media technologies and patterns of consumption and response
- how audiences interpret the media, including how they may interpret the same media in different ways
- how audiences interact with the media and can be actively involved in media production.

For further information on audience theories and ideas, see Chapter 5 in the Year 1 & AS Media Studies student book.

Media audiences

REVISION BOOSTER

Media audiences need to be considered in these four ways:

1 The importance of target audiences for media producers
2 The way audiences use the media – their motivations and behaviours
3 The potential effects of the media on audiences
4 The impact of technology on audiences

3.1 The importance of target audiences for media producers

Every media product needs an audience. Without an audience the media product will fail as it will not be able to generate an income. Before a media product is created, media producers need to define who they assume the audience would be, so they can try to create something that will attract an audience and then maintain, and hopefully, extend it.

Target audiences can be defined by:

- **Demographics:** by identifiable groupings within society.
- **Psychographics:** by the interests and values of groups of people.

Demographics

Audience members are part of specific groups within society. These groups are divided by age, gender and social/economic class.

Name some media products that target their audience by demographics and how this group is targeted.

Demographic group	Media product	How it attempts to please the target audience
Age	*Countdown* (Channel 4)	A slow-paced puzzle game that plays on the stereotype that this would be of interest to older audiences. It is broadcast in the afternoon when retirees may be watching.
Age	*Hollyoaks* (Channel 4)	
Age		
Gender	www.glamourmagazine.co.uk	*Glamour* magazine targets females by presenting topics that are stereotypically of interest to women – fashion, beauty, celebrity gossip, etc.
Gender	www.gq-magazine.co.uk	
Gender		
Social class/ wealth	www.gq-magazine.co.uk	*GQ* magazine targets 'young professionals', promoting a lifestyle that values sophisticated fashion with some luxurious elements.
Social class/ wealth	www.glamourmagazine.co.uk	
Social class/ wealth		

Psychographics

Here are three types of audience taken from the VALs* psychographic framework:

A **Reformers:** people who want their choices to have a positive impact on the world. They may be political and often consider the broader impact of the things they do.

B **Aspirers:** people who like to be at the cutting edge of fashion, technology and culture. They like to see themselves as trend-setters.

C **Experiencers:** people who enjoy activities and they see themselves as active outgoing people.

(*VALs categories can be found at: **www.strategicbusinessinsights.com/ vals/ustypes.shtml**)

 ACTIVITY 3.2 Imagine you are creating a food channel for YouTube. Your content will contain recipes and discussions on nutrition, diets and other food-related topics. You plan to make different types of videos to appeal that different audiences. Describe the content of videos that aim to appeal to the following groups:

Reformers	Aspirers	Experiencers

 TIP There are many different approaches to psychographics. It doesn't matter which approach you have studied as long as you can apply the principals of appealing to audiences based on their interests and values.

Media producers don't actually mind who their **actual audience** is – just having an audience is enough. However, having a clear idea as to who the **target audience** is benefits the producer in a number of ways.

ACTIVITY 3.3 How does having a clear target audience help media producers? Consider how this helps with production, distribution and the circulation of a media product.

Production	Distribution	Circulation

There are many different ideas about audiences, but following are the ideas that you **need** to know and understand for the examination.

ESSENTIAL AUDIENCE TERMS AND IDEAS

Ideas about the way audiences use the media

Reception theory:
- agenda setting
- framing
- myth making
- conditions of consumption.

Hall's ideas and theories on reception theory:
- encoding/decoding
- hegemonic/negotiated/oppositional.

Ideas about the potential impact of the media on audiences

Media effects:
- uses and gratifications
- hypodermic needle theory
- moral panic
- cumulation
- media literacy.

Bandura's ideas and theories on media effects:
- social learning/imitation.

Cultivation theory:
- socialisation
- standardisation
- enculturation
- bardic function.

Gerbner's ideas and theories on cultivation theory:
- resonance
- mean world index/syndrome.

3.2 The way audiences use the media – their motivations and behaviours

You have already looked at some of the ideas about audience engagement with the media in the media language section (see Activity 1.4).

Audiences **decode** the media language choices encoded by media producers to make meaning. However, we don't all interpret the media in the same way. Many factors can alter the **decoding** and **reception** of a media product. Producers try to control the reception of their product in the choices they make during construction.

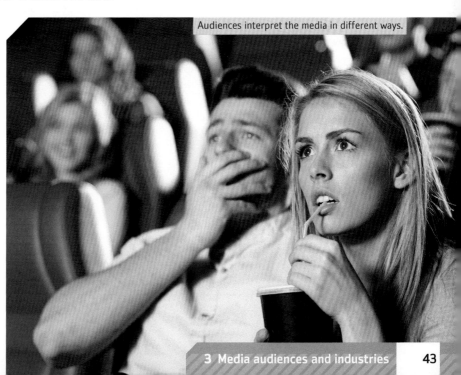

Audiences interpret the media in different ways.

Look at the following terms and their meanings.

Term	Meaning	Techniques demonstrated in Activity 2.3 Newspapers
Agenda setting	Presenting information in such a way as to influence the perception of its importance.	
Framing	Presenting information with a specific focus on certain parts rather than presenting the whole story or a complete image. Framing can also take place by presenting information using a specific tone or with an identifiable attitude.	
Myth making	The repetition of or construction of popular ideas as if they are 'normal' or 'natural' when they represent a specific (and debatable) point of view.	

1   How do the examples of the newspaper front pages provided for Activity 2.3 demonstrate the use of these techniques? Write your answers in the third column of the above table.

2   How does *Psychologies Magazine* set an agenda and frame the information it is presenting?

Audiences may find that both internal and external forces can impact on the reception of a media product. A person's personality, personal value system, age, nationality and gender could influence the way they receive and interpret media messages. External forces may also have an impact.

How might the following **conditions of consumption** impact on the reception of media products?

Conditions of consumption	Impact
Going to the cinema with a large friend group to watch a horror film.	
Sitting at home alone watching a horror film on a tablet or computer.	
Reading a newspaper at home alone.	
Reading a news app on a noisy bus.	

3.3 The potential effects of the media on audiences

This is one of the most debated aspects of the theoretical framework. Some people fear that the media can have a negative impact on the audience and may act to alter an individual's attitudes and behaviours. Other people question the assumptions made about the power of the media, saying that audience members often control their own media consumption and are not all affected by the media in the same way.

 ACTIVITY 3.6 Define the following ideas about audiences and show which ideas see the audience as passive and which see the audience as active. How relevant do you think these ideas are? What are the arguments for and/or against the theories?

Theory	Definition	Active and/or passive	Arguments for and/or against this theory
Social learning theory (Bandura)			
Hypodermic needle theory			
Uses and gratifications theory			
Media literacy			
Cumulative effects theory			

The problem with effects theories is that it is difficult to prove the effects of the media on individuals or larger groups. One idea that aims to show the media can have an effect is the idea of **moral panic**. Moral panics are when a problem is identified as being a moral threat to society. Sometimes, moral panics are focused on groups of people (e.g. youths, immigrants) but often they are focused on specific areas of the media itself – specifically, new media forms and technologies.

ACTIVITY 3.7

Identify which of the following media forms/areas have generated moral panics:

		Yes	No			Yes	No			Yes	No
a	film	☐	☐	e	horror films	☐	☐	i	the news	☐	☐
b	comic books	☐	☐	f	gaming	☐	☐	j	social media.	☐	☐
c	radio	☐	☐	g	newspapers	☐	☐				
d	rock and roll	☐	☐	h	violent films	☐	☐				

Cultivation theory

Cultivation theory discusses the potential long-term effects of the media. Rather than having an immediate effect, the effect on the audience is something that develops over time. Specifically, cultivation theory argues that the media can shape the way people see the world.

ACTIVITY 3.8

1 Consider the qualities that are deemed 'attractive' or 'beautiful' in today's culture.

List the places where the media represents ideas about physical attractiveness for women and for men.

Ideas of attractiveness for men are represented here:	Ideas of attractiveness for women are represented here:
Men's Health magazine	TeenVogue.com
Love Island	Perfume adverts

2 Apply cultivation theory by discussing how the repetition of specific ideas of what is attractive could impact on media audiences over time.

ACTIVITY 3.9 Use the following words to complete this description of key ideas from cultivation theory. Each one is used once.

standardised

mainstreaming

enculturation

resonance

mean world index

cultivates

socialisation

cultivation differential

bardic function

The media can have an impact on the way people **learn about the norms and values of the surrounding culture**. Along with family, friends and education, the media can impact on the _____ of a person. The media reproduces the norms about the producing culture and these values become part of the way a person **learns to behave and interact with others**. This is called the _____ process. Social roles and norms are _____ in media representations. The media _____ attitudes and values that fit in with the dominant ideologies of the culture.

Hartley and Fiske argue that the media has a _____ _____ for audiences **acting to tell the stories that help communicate the fears, concerns and preoccupations of the producing culture**. Media products also generate their own 'realities'. Studies showed that **the more a person accessed the media, the more they absorbed the ideas being communicated**. The difference between light users and heavy users is called the _____ _____. Where messages in the media **relate to the audience's experiences** they are said to have _____. This allows the _____ of these ideas. This is the process that means that **heavy media users from different social groups tend to have a similar world view** that reflects the views communicated across the media. Often the ideas communicated by the media are very negative. **People often think the world is a more dangerous and violent place than it really is**. This is called the _____ _____.

3.4 The impact of technology on audiences

Modern technologies have impacted on the conditions of consumption for audiences. Audience behaviours and responses have also adapted as the technologies we use have developed. Audiences can interact with media producers and other audience members. In the past, audiences could only be receivers of information, but they can now also send information.

ACTIVITY 3.10

1 How do the following media forms allow audience interaction with producers and with other audience members?

Media form	Interaction with producers	Interaction with audience members
Newspapers		
Radio		
Television		
Gaming		
Magazines		
Film		

2 How might interaction with producers give the audience power and help them influence production choices?

3 How might interaction with other audience members influence a person's response to a media product?

Media audiences are also able to become media producers. Technological developments have meant that anyone with a smartphone and an internet connection can create media content. This may involve complex skills such as filming and editing a video for YouTube or creating written content as part of an online discussion.

How can audiences contribute content to existing media products and how can they create their own media products related to the listed media forms?

Media form	Contributions to media products	Creation of their own media products
Newspapers		
Radio		
Television		
Gaming		
Magazines		
Film		

SUMMARY

Audiences

- Media producers need to create products that **appeal** to audiences.
- Media products are created by focusing on the perceived **interests and expectations** of the **target audience**.
- Audiences **interpret** the messages communicated by media products.
- They may not always accept the producer's **intended meaning**.
- There are concerns about the **possible (negative) effects** of the media on audiences.
- **Audience behaviours** alter as technologies develop.
- Modern audiences often **contribute** to and **interact** with media products.
- Modern audiences are often **participants** rather than just passive observers.

Media industries

SPEC SPOTLIGHT

This is from the AQA specification:

In this section students will develop their knowledge and understanding of:

- processes of production, distribution and circulation by organisations, groups and individuals in a global context
- the specialised and institutionalised nature of media production, distribution and circulation
- the relationship of recent technological change and media production, distribution and circulation
- the significance of patterns of ownership and control, including conglomerate ownership, vertical integration and diversification
- the significance of economic factors, including commercial and not-for-profit public funding, to media industries and their products
- how media organisations maintain, including through marketing, varieties of audiences nationally and globally
- the regulatory framework of contemporary media in the UK
- the impact of 'new' digital technologies on media regulation, including the role of individual producers.

Introduction

The final area of the theoretical framework is the study of Media Industries. This area of the framework considers ideas relating to the organisations, businesses and individuals that create media products. As different media industries work in different ways, it is often easier to understand the nature of specific industries as they are linked to the CSPs. This chapter will help you to revise industry ideas and concepts. These concepts need to be applied to the CSPs using the specific industrial context of each product. Strategies for doing this will be dealt with in Chapters 4 and 5 of this book.

> ∞ Further information on media industries and discussion on all the terms and ideas can be found in Chapter 6 of the Year 1 & AS student book.

REVISION BOOSTER

The study of media industries breaks down into three key areas:

1 Funding
2 Production, distribution and circulation
3 Regulation/ownership and control

There are many different ideas about industry but following are the ideas that you **need** to know and understand for the examination.

ESSENTIAL INDUSTRY TERMS AND IDEAS

Power and media industries as summarised by Curran and Seaton:

- regulation
- deregulation
- free market
- media concentration
- PSB
- globalisation
- conglomerates
- neo-liberalism
- surveillance
- privacy
- security.

Vlogging is a new type of media industry.

3.5 Funding

Media industries need money to be able to make media products. Media products in turn offer opportunities for media industries to generate a profit, as long as an audience can be found for them.

You will need to consider:

- How are media industries funded?
- How do media industries generate money?

Funding models

ACTIVITY 3.12

There are several different models of funding used by media industries.

1 Describe what is meant by each model.
2 Identify some British media industries that use the following models.

Model	Meaning	British example
The commercial model	Income is generated by selling space or time to advertisers.	
The public service model		The BBC
The mixed model (commercial and public service)		
The subscription model	Income is generated by audience members paying a regular (often monthly) fee to allow them to access content.	
The 'pay-per-view' model		Sky Sports

Many industries use a mixed model of some sort. The BBC cannot show adverts on its UK-based broadcast and streaming platforms, but this is not the case where it broadcasts in the US using its subscription- and advert-funded BBC America channel

To help control expenses and income, many large media companies use **vertical integration**, when the company runs two or more of the various stages of production. For example, a magazine producer that owns printing plants and transportation companies can control the content, the physical production and the distribution of the magazine.

All media industries try to maximise their incomes, so many use different media platforms that allow for different income streams. This is called **diversification**. Media products themselves can generate income in different ways, which is something industries try to capitalise on.

The BBC cannot show adverts in the UK.

Generating income

1 Identify some of the ways that media products make money.

2 Consider the ways that the media forms can generate an income. There will probably be several income streams for each media form. List as many as you can.

Media form	Income streams
Television programmes	In-programme advertising; product placement; DVD/digital download sales; international sales; franchising spin-offs; merchandising; cross-media tie-ins (e.g. apps, websites, etc.); licencing to streaming services.
Film	
Newspapers	
Magazines	
Online magazines/ news sites	
Computer games	
Radio	

3 Why do media industries often decide to **diversify** – that is, create different media products and forms across multiple platforms? What are the benefits of **diversification**?

ACTIVITY 3.14

There have been some controversies over the way that digital media can create targeted advertising for each individual user. Using the following three terms, write a paragraph explaining why the use of online data to present personalised advertising for each user is sometimes thought to be a problem.

surveillance   privacy   security

3.6 Production, distribution and circulation

Media industries are involved in three main processes: production, distribution and circulation.

ACTIVITY 3.15

Define these terms:

1 **Production** is ...
2 **Distribution** is ...
3 **Circulation** is ...

Production

The budgets available to spend on production will impact on the way a media product looks and the audience's experiences.

ACTIVITY 3.16

Discuss the differences you may expect between low-budget and high-budget productions in these forms.

Media form	Production differences
Film	Limited use of studio sets for filming; lesser known actors cast in lead roles; limited use of special effects.
Magazines	
Music video	
Newspapers	
Radio	
Television	
Gaming	

Distribution

Getting the media product to the audience can use both traditional and new digital methods. Some traditional methods are becoming less popular with audiences and digital distribution is often cheaper and more convenient for both media industries and audiences.

Consider the media forms in the following table.
1 What are the traditional methods of distributing each form?
2 What are the newer methods used to distribute each form?
3 What are the benefits for the audience and for the producer for each of these methods?

Form	Traditional distribution methods	Benefits for the audience and/or producer	Newer distribution methods	Benefits for the audience and/or producer
Television programming				
Magazines				
Music videos				

Circulation

A media product cannot be successful if its audience don't know about it. Media producers try to maximise the circulation of their product – that is, get as many people as possible watching, reading and/or listening to the product. Modern audiences can be difficult to find – the variety of distribution methods available today means that audiences have a lot of control over when and how they access media products. Trailers played on TV, film trailers at the cinema and adverts in magazines rely on traditional audience behaviours to promote a media product. Digital and social media have altered audience behaviours and the way media products are promoted.

ACTIVITY 3.18

Using social and/or digital media, how might a media industry try to promote the following new media products?

1 A new low-budget horror film being shown at some film festivals and available on Vimeo.

3 A new reality TV show shown on a streaming service such as Netflix.

2 A new virtual reality gaming website.

4 A new musical artist.

3.7 Regulation/ownership and control

In a **free market**, a media product's success will always be determined by reaching an audience and generating a profit. Media products that fail will disappear and be replaced by ones that the audience want to see, read or listen to.

Some argue that to be a truly **neo-liberal free market**, media industries should be free from regulation, and the success or not of a media product should be determined by the market – the audience.

Regulation

In order to protect the public, media industries are regulated. This stops media industries exploiting audiences in ways that may be seen to be immoral or inappropriate. Different industries have different regulators but they all provide codes that govern the way media industries behave.

1 Which media industries are regulated by the following organisations? Identify some of the regulations these organisations place on media industries.

2 What are the arguments for regulation of the media?

3 Why is online media difficult to regulate? Consider the globalised nature of the internet.

4 What arguments could be put forward for the deregulation of traditional media since the growth of online and digital media platforms?

ACTIVITY
3.20

1 Another aspect of the ideal of the **free market** is fair competition. How might the following media industries have an advantage over other media industries?

a International conglomerates such as Hearst Communications.

b Public service broadcasters such as the BBC.

2 Much of the world's media is owned by a small number of massive media corporations. This concentration of ownership is often criticised. What problems might the concentration of ownership cause?

Individual producers

Traditionally, media industries had to be large, wealthy corporations, as producing media content was expensive and time-consuming. Digital technologies have provided easier access to the ability to produce, distribute and circulate media productions.

Production and distribution

ACTIVITY
3.21

What technology do you need access to in order to be able to do the following?

Start a 'lifestyle' YouTube channel	
Create music and upload to Soundcloud	
Create an Instagram account presenting images and ideas about health and fitness	
Create a blog on which you analyse and comment on current news and politics	

Individuals are able to access **production** and **distribution** technologies, and many individuals have become media producers. However, just providing content does not necessarily mean that people will watch, read or listen to what is being created. Circulation is still very difficult for individuals who do not have a marketing budget or the contacts and connections that help traditional media industries get their content in front of large audiences.

Circulation

ACTIVITY 3.22

What methods can media industries use to promote the following media products?

A 'lifestyle' YouTube channel	
An artist whose music is available on Soundcloud	
A health and fitness-based Instagram account	
A news and politics blog	

SUMMARY

Industry

- Media industries are **funded** and/or **generate income** in a number of different ways.
- Media industries are involved in the **production, distribution and circulation** of media products.
- Media products are only successful when they find and appeal to an audience.
- Traditional media industries are having to **adapt to use modern technologies** to meet audience needs.
- Media producers can be very powerful, so the media is **regulated**.
- Digital technologies mean that **individuals can produce and distribute** media products.

Chapter 4

Targeted close study products: exam Section A

Introduction to close study products

Over the course of the year you will have studied nine close study products (CSPs). These are the media products identified by the exam board, which cover nine media forms. The idea of the CSPs is that they will help you to provide evidence for the ideas and concepts you have learned in your study of the theoretical framework.

The CSPs are divided into two different types – targeted CSPs and in-depth CSPs.

Targeted CSPs

- Studied using selected areas of the theoretical framework.
- Assessed in **Sections A and B** of the exam.

Section A

To be studied using media language and representation ideas.

- Gaming: Tomb Raider: Anniversary (2007).
- Magazines: specific pages from *Men's Health* magazine, as published in the exam board's CSP guidance booklet.
- Advertising and marketing: Maybelline: *That Boss Life part 1*.

Section B

To be studied using audience and industry ideas:

- Television: *Deutschland 83* (Series 1, Episode 1), *The Missing* (Series 2, Episode 1) OR *The Killing* (Series 1, Episode 1).
- Music video: Common: *Letter to the Free*.

To be studied using Industry ideas:

- Film: *Hidden Figures*.

A screenshot from Common's *Letter to the Free* video

In depth CSPs

Studied using all areas of the theoretical framework.

Assessed in Section C of the exam

The current in depth CSPs are:

- Radio: *The War of the Worlds* (1938).
- Newspapers: specific pages from the *i* as published in the exam board's CSP guidance booklet.
- Online, social and participatory media: TeenVogue.com.

REVISION BOOSTER

Always check the most up-to-date information on CSPs published by the exam board to make sure you are studying the correct products, using the correct areas of the theoretical framework.

You will need to know all the CSPs well as you may be asked to discuss any of them in the exam. This means you should be familiar with each media product and you need to read, watch and listen to them multiple times before the exam. When you answer questions in the exam, you will need to use your detailed knowledge of the products to demonstrate how ideas from the theoretical framework can be applied. You also need to use specific examples from the CSPs. You can use the CSPs to help you revise the theoretical framework.

This chapter offers revision ideas and strategies for three of the targeted CSPs covering advertising and marketing, television and film.

In order to effectively revise for the examination, you should consider the CSPs in light of the appropriate areas of the theoretical framework. Many of the following activities can be adapted for use with other CSPs to help when revising for the examination. When revising, you should use the CSPs to help you revise the theoretical framework. Practise using theoretical ideas and the specialist terminology you have learned to discuss all the CSPs. The activities that follow are constructed to create lots of opportunities for you to think about and engage with the theoretical concepts and the enabling ideas set by the exam board. They should also encourage you to make sure you are using examples from the CSPs to support your ideas and to show how they work.

Chapters 1–3 provided activities that should have helped you develop your theoretical knowledge and understanding. Chapters 4 and 5 will help you apply the ideas and develop your knowledge of the selected CSPs.

Both of the Media Studies student books contain information on a number of CSPs. See the table on page 6 of this revision guide to see where you can read about additional CSPs.

4.1 Close study product 1: Maybelline: *That Boss Life part 1*

Media form: Advertising and marketing

Targeted areas of the theoretical framework: media language and representations

The video can be found on YouTube: www.youtube.com/watch?v=PfJD5i3yIdM.

Media form

When preparing to revise any media product it is a good idea to start by identifying formally what it is and what it is for.

ACTIVITY 4.1

Identify the form and function of *That Boss Life part 1*.

1 Media form?

a Film

b Advertising and marketing

c Television

2 Method of production?

a Audio

b Moving image

c Print

3 Method of distribution?

a Television   c Online

b Cinema   d Radio

4 What is the main function of this product?

a To provide information.

b To entertain the audience.

c To persuade the audience to do something.

d To create a personal communication with the audience.

This information will help you to decide why certain production decisions have been made. The focus of your study here is **media language** and **representations**. You should be considering the choices that have been made in production and the way the media language combines to create meaning. You also need to consider the context of this advert, which may mean you will want to make connections to ideas about audience and industry when revising for the exam. Audience and industry are not the main focus of your study of this advert but they are part of the CSP's context.

Media language/semiotics

Media language analysis

1 Identify media language choices that have been made in the production of the Maybelline *That Boss Life part 1* advert. At first, focus on **denotations**. As you don't know what you will be asked in the exam it is a good idea to consider a range of different media language choices. In the following table, identify as many examples of the media language choices made in its production as you can and use specialist terminology when making your observations.

Cinematography (use of camera)	Editing	Sound	Mise-en-scène (including lighting)	Special effects
Wide shots to show the location outside the window.	Slow editing style.	Upbeat modern music.	Casting: a male and a female YouTube celebrity.	The use of light flares.

(Continued)

2 Select three of your observations and think about why these choices may have been made. What **connotations** do these choices create? What is the intended effect of each choice?

Media language observation	Why was this chosen?	What connotations are created?	What is the intended effect of this choice?
Upbeat modern music.	To appeal to a modern, young audience.	The advert appears up to date and the music connotes ideas of parties, socialising, etc.	To create a positive and happy tone that can be associated with the brand/product.

The producers of the advert have carefully considered each media language choice in its construction. Every choice is intended to work with the other choices in combination, to make meaning. This advert wants to present the mascara in as positive a way as possible and, ultimately, persuade the audience to select and buy this brand of mascara rather than all the others on offer.

Media language creates representations

ACTIVITY
4.3

Answer the following questions in the table below.

1 Identify media language choices that have been selected to show the mascara in a positive way.

2 Identify media language choices that have been selected to show the brand (Maybelline) in a positive way.

3 Identify how media language has been used to attempt to persuade the audience to select this mascara.

Media language to promote the mascara	Media language to create a positive brand image	Media language for persuasion

Semiotics

You can use the advert to help you revise semiotic terminology.

ACTIVITY
4.4

1 Using examples from *That Boss Life part 1*, complete the following to show your knowledge and understanding of both semiotic terms and the advert's construction.

a _____ is an example of an icon.

b _____ is an example of an index.

c _____ is an example of a symbol.

d _____ is used to create anchorage.

Signs are used as signifiers of ideas (the signified).

2 Identify three signs used in the Maybelline advert and what ideas they signify.

a Sign 1 _____ signifies _____ .

b Sign 2 _____ signifies _____ .

c Sign 3 _____ signifies _____ .

Creating messages

ACTIVITY
4.5

Write a brief (10- to 15-minute response) to the following question:

- *That Boss Life part 1* uses carefully chosen media language choices to communicate its messages to the audience. What messages and ideologies are being communicated in the advert? Use specific examples of media language to show how these ideas are communicated.

Media language – genre

That Boss Life part 1 is an advert. It is part of the **genre** of beauty adverts and in the **sub-genre** of mascara adverts. Beauty adverts are one of the many **genres** of advertising, so there are **codes** and **conventions** expected of this type of advertising that are different from the codes and conventions of other genres.

Genre

ACTIVITY 4.6

Look at the two adverts on the left. What genre of advert are they and in what ways are they typical of the genre?

Advert	Genre of advert	How this advert is typical of the genre
Thomson		
Tesco		

ACTIVITY 4.7

What are the codes and conventions of modern cosmetic adverts? Does the Maybelline advert follow conventions, subvert them or does it do both?

Codes and conventions of cosmetic advertising	*That Boss Life part 1* – examples of it following conventions	Why it follows these conventions	*That Boss Life part 1* – examples of it subverting conventions	Why it subverts these conventions

That Boss Life part 1 is an example of a beauty advert, but it is also an advert for mascara. Mascara, lipstick, shampoo and face cream are all beauty products, but they all follow their own advertising conventions. They are all sub-genres of beauty advertising.

To be able to consider the advert as part of the **sub-genre** of mascara adverts, you will need to be familiar with other examples from the sub-genre. You can watch other mascara adverts on YouTube, for example:

- *L'Oréal Paris Mega Volume Miss Manga Mascara Official TV Advert*: www.youtube.com/watch?v=5ZiMbdyisvk
- *Avon TV Advert / Big & ExtremeMascara*: www.youtube.com/watch?v=O58P5A5K_e0
- *Max Factor False Lash Effect Fusion Mascara Advert*: www.youtube.com/watch?v=2kuocCZCZYc.

Genre: codes and conventions

ACTIVITY
4.8

Is *That Boss Life part 1* a typical mascara advert? In the table below, identify the media language choices that follow the sub-genre's codes and conventions and the media language choices that subvert them.

A still from an Avon mascara advert

Codes and conventions of mascara adverts	*That Boss Life part 1* – examples of it following conventions	Why does it follow these conventions?	*That Boss Life part 1* – examples of it subverting conventions	Why does it subvert these conventions?

You also know that genres need to **adapt** and **change** to ensure that they continue to interest and engage their target audience.

A collection of historical Maybelline cosmetic adverts, *Vintage Maybelline Commercials*, can be seen on YouTube: www.youtube.com/watch?v=eJCnr5kaps8.

Genre development and change

ACTIVITY 4.9

Has cosmetics/mascara advertising changed over the years?

Similar, yet different: (left) a vintage Maybelline advert; (right) a still from the *That Boss Life part 1* advert

Ways the genre/sub-genre has stayed the same	What is the significance of the codes and conventions that have stayed the same?	Ways the genre/sub-genre has changed	Why do you think the genre/sub-genre has changed over the years?

Modern examples of any genre need to be relevant for contemporary audiences.

Media language creates audience appeal

ACTIVITY 4.10

Identify the specific media language choices/codes and conventions used in the *That Boss Life part 1* advert in an attempt to appeal to contemporary viewers.

Media language and narrative

Most adverts use the same basic narrative: a problem is identified and a **solution** offered. The solution is, of course, related to the product being promoted in the advert. This is the basis of advertising, as producers want to create a problem that the audience would like to solve and then immediately offer them the solution.

This is very similar to Todorov's narrative structure. Todorov says that most narratives begin with an **equilibrium** that is disrupted by some sort of problem. The story is based on attempts to solve the problem and a new **equilibrium** is created when the problem has been resolved. In advertising, the new equilibrium is established once the product has ended the **disruption** or solved the problem. In a short advert like *That Boss Life part 1* the producers don't have time to develop these stages of the narrative in any great detail, so they have to communicate the idea quickly in an often simplistic way. It is worth noting that the advert is identified as 'part 1' of a story, so it may not offer a full new equilibrium, as the story is continued in 'part 2'.

That Boss Life part 2 ft. MannyMua and Makeupshayla / New Big Shot Mascara, which can be viewed at: www.youtube.com/watch?v=4yFWpVo85_0.

1 Complete the following about *That Boss Life part 1*:

a The equilibrium in the world of the advert is: _____.

b Disruption/the problem identified in the advert is: _____.

c The new equilibrium shown in the advert is: _____.

2 Now you need to identify how the advert creates and communicates the narrative. How is media language used to communicate the idea of:

Equilibrium	Disruption	New equilibrium

Equilibrium is established, disrupted but then improved and restored.

The advert may be less than one minute long, but it does tell a brief story and has a simple plot.

Plot

ACTIVITY 4.12

Summarise the story being told by the advert. You can use full sentences or bullet points if you prefer.

Although the plot is very simple, it is an example of a masterplot – one of the types of stories that are repeated over and over across time and in many different media forms.

Masterplot

ACTIVITY 4.13

Tick which of the following masterplots best defines the *That Boss Life part 1* advert?

1 The revenge narrative: the protagonist's goal is to seek out people who have done something terrible and then impart their own version of justice. ☐

2 The coming of age narrative: the protagonist has experiences that cause them to grow from being a child into a young adult. ☐

3 The transformation narrative: experiences allow the protagonist to change – usually for the better. ☐

Their world is transformed.

Manny and Makeupshayla's experience is **transformed** by the mascara. There is a **causality** between the mascara and the more glamorous world shown at the end of the advert.

Media language is used to provide information that helps the audience to understand the narrative. Media language is **diegetic** – as it points out information that the producers see as important.

Narrative codes

ACTIVITY 4.14

How is media language used to:

a   indicate where the advert is set (both inside the room and outside)

b   indicate when the advert is set (the past, the present, the future)

c   show the difference in status between the stars of the advert and the bell boy

d   demonstrate the 'appropriate response' to the mascara

e   demonstrate the 'appropriate response' to the world being represented

f   communicate the brand identity?

The advert also uses narrative roles (Propp) within its story.

Here are some conventional
narrative roles:

Hero   Villain   Doner

Helper   Dispatcher

The mascara

Narrative roles

ACTIVITY 4.15

1   Which role does Shayla play when she says, 'You know what, let's get bossed up'?

2   Which role does Manny play when he opens the suitcase, presents the contents to Shayla and nods?

3   Which role does the mascara play in the story?

4   How can the actions of the bell boy towards the end of the advert be seen to fit in (very briefly) with another narrative role?

Representations

Representations are created by combining media language choices together. The advert creates a number of representations.

Manny and Shayla are represented as individuals but they also act as representations of the groups they are part of. Manny and Shayla can be seen as representations of their race, gender and sexuality. They are also representations of:

- make-up artists
- celebrities – specifically YouTube stars
- youth and youth culture
- a glamorous lifestyle.

As adverts have to tell their stories very quickly, they often rely on stereotypes to help them create quick, simple-to-understand messages. The audience's interpretation of these representations often relate to contemporary ideologies and values. All representations are **selective** and they construct a **version of reality**.

ACTIVITY 4.16

1 What stereotypes/stereotypical ideas have been used in the advert? Do you think these stereotypes create positive or negative messages?

2 What are the values of the advert? What ideologies does the advert communicate?

3 Considering your responses to the above questions, now identify the way the producers encode these messages.

The messages created by media products are influenced by the dominant ideologies of the producing culture. Some of the messages created in advertising reflect the ideas and values that the audience feel are true (or maybe just want to be true).

Representation and ideology

ACTIVITY 4.17

1 Which of these statements about contemporary culture do you think are supported by the representations created in the production of the advert?

	Yes	No
a A glamorous lifestyle is only available to people who have wealthy parents.	☐	☐
b Men should be tough.	☐	☐
c Cities are dangerous, violent places.	☐	☐
d Different races can all be beautiful.	☐	☐
e A person's sexuality is not important.	☐	☐
f Make-up can make your life more exciting and fashionable.	☐	☐

2 Are the ideas created by the advert accurate? Would they represent the audience's lived experience?

Although the representations within advertising may not always be accurate and may contain many **mis-representations**, advertising works by selling ideas and ideals. Audiences may feel that while they can't access the prestigious lifestyle portrayed here, buying the mascara may help them feel they can experience a small part of it.

Identity

The advert subverts conventional ideas of gender, as Manny is a male make-up artist who also wears make-up himself. Modern culture consists of lots of different people who have differing ideas and values, and, in some areas of modern culture, gender identity is seen to be more fluid and less fixed. The advert is in some ways conventional in its representation of gender identity, but in other ways it communicates very modern values.

Gender identity

ACTIVITY 4.18

List the ways that gender is represented conventionally and how it is represented in a more fluid, modern way. Focus on media language choices and representations.

Conventional ideas of gender identity in the advert	Ideas about gender fluidity in the advert
Manny provides the means for transformation.	Manny wears make-up.

Context

Industry/audience

It is important to remember that this is a modern advertising product. Advertisers always research their target audience, so they can make choices that will appeal to them to help make their advertising campaigns more successful. Although the focus of this targeted CSP is media language and representation, it's important to note that all the media language choices are made because it is assumed they will help sell the mascara to the audience. Advertising needs to be persuasive if it is to be successful.

Online advertising

The Boss Life advert features YouTube celebrities and was intended to be shown online. Online advertising often relies on gaining more attention through **going viral** by encouraging the audience to get involved by sharing the advert. The casting of Manny and Shayla shows how a well-established make-up brand is trying to update its **brand identity** and appeal to a contemporary audience.

The advert in its YouTube context.

ACTIVITY 4.19

1 Identify the way media language choices and representations are used to try to create a modern brand identity for Maybelline.

2 How does the casting of Manny and Shayla help Maybelline reach more audience members?

Summary: *That Boss Life part 1*

ACTIVITY 4.20

To summarise your study of *That Boss Life part 1* discuss the way the advert uses media language choices and the construction of representations to attempt to persuade the audience to desire, and hopefully buy, the mascara.

- Use specific examples from the advert and describe them using media language terms.
- Use semiotic terminology to explain how meaning is created.
- Use ideas about representation and identity to explain how the advert is trying to fulfil its function and appeal to its audience.

OVER THE WALL.
UNDER THE GUN.

DEUTSCHLAND 83

4.2 Close study product 2: *Deutschland 83*: Series 1, Episode 1

Media form: Television

Targeted areas of the theoretical framework: audience and industry

REVISION BOOSTER

This CSP needs to be looked at using ideas from the audience and industry areas of the theoretical framework. In order to discuss ideas such as audience appeal it could be necessary to refer to specific uses of media language, the use of genre, and narrative codes and representations constructed by the television programme. This means that you will need to be familiar with the first episode of the first series of *Deutschland 83*. You will also need to be familiar with the marketing products used to promote the programme, including trailers, posters and social media activity.

Some knowledge of the industrial context of the television programme is necessary and you should be able to use this information to show your knowledge and understanding of industry issues and debates.

Form and function

When preparing to revise any media product it is a good idea to start by identifying formally what it is and what it is for.

ACTIVITY 4.21

Identify the form and function of *Deutschland 83*.

1 Media form?

  a Film

  b Advertising and marketing

  c Television

2 Method of production?

  a Audio

  b Moving image

  c Print

3 Method of distribution?

  a Television   c Online

  b Cinema   d Radio

4 What is the main function of this product?

  a To provide information.

  b To entertain the audience.

  c To persuade the audience to do something.

  d To create a personal communication with the audience.

Introduction activities

Genre

ACTIVITY 4.22

1 How would you define the **genre** of *Deutschland 83*? Explain the reasons for your definition.

2 Using details from the first episode, demonstrate how the programme can be seen as:

  a a spy thriller

  b a coming of age drama

  c a costume drama

  d a political drama

  e a military drama.

An indication of genre?

Narrative

1   Write a brief **plot summary** of the episode. What happens in it?

2   What roles do the following **characters** play in the **narrative** of the first episode?

Martin and Lenora

Character	Role in the plot	Narrative role (Propp)
Martin Rauch		
General Edel		
Anett Schneider		
Ingrid Rauch		
Leonora Rauch		

3   How is the **narrative structured** in the first episode?

How does the episode identify the equilibrium?	How is the equilibrium disrupted?	Is there a sense of a new equilibrium at the end of the episode?

Media language

Identify some uses of media language that you found interesting in the first episode.

Media language	Your observations: what did you see and what effects were created?
Cinematography	
Editing	
Sound and music	
Mise-en-scène (including lighting)	
Special effects	

Stylised cinematography

Representations

When watching the first episode, what struck you about the representations of the following?

	Notes on the representations
Martin Rauch	
Anett Schneider	
General Edel	
Leonora Rauch	
Ingrid Rauch	
East Germany	
West Germany	
The 1980s	
The Cold War	

Industry

Deutschland 83 is a German-language television programme. It was produced in Germany by **UFA GmbH** and was partially funded by **Sundance TV**. The programme was initially broadcast in Germany on **RTL**. It was distributed globally by **Freemantle Media International** and was broadcast by **Channel 4** in the UK in January 2016 – it is still available to watch within the **Walter Presents** area of **All 4**, Channel 4's streaming service. Walter Presents is a curated collection of non-English language television programmes available to stream online. Channel 4 expanded its non-English-language programming after the success on BBC 4 of the Danish crime drama *The Killing*.

Regulation

The content of all television programmes in the UK is regulated by Ofcom.

Read the following taken from the Ofcom website:

What is the watershed?

10 May 2013

Protecting children from harmful material on TV and radio is one of Ofcom's most important duties.

Our Broadcasting Code sets standards for television and radio shows and broadcasters must follow its rules.

Our Broadcasting Code sets standards for television and radio shows and broadcasters must follow its rules.

There are strict rules about what can be shown on TV before the 9pm watershed. But what exactly is the watershed and how does it work?

The watershed means the time when TV programmes which might be unsuitable for children can be broadcast.

When is it?

The watershed begins at 9pm and material unsuitable for children should not, in general, be shown before 9pm or after 5.30am.

What do you mean by unsuitable material?

Unsuitable material can include everything from sexual content to violence, graphic or distressing images and swearing. For example, the most offensive language must not be broadcast before the watershed on TV, or on radio, when children are particularly likely to be listening. Frequent use of offensive language must be avoided before the watershed, and must always be justified by its context.

More information can be found on the Ofcom website: www.ofcom.org.uk/.

1 Why is the content of TV programming regulated?

2 *Deutschland 83* does have some content that would not be appropriate for children. How would Channel 4 make sure that it was following the regulations about making sure small children did not have access to this programme?

3 It is harder to regulate programming on streaming services. How does Channel 4 try to ensure that children do not have access to violent, sexual or potentially disturbing images?

Production and distribution

Some information first:

- **UFA** is a German film and television production company. It is part of the RTL group – a subsidiary of Bertelsmann – one of the largest media conglomerates in the world. Bertelsmann owns (among other companies) Penguin Random House book publishers, Gruner and Jahr magazine publisher, a printing company and the music publishing company BMG. UFA owns production studios. During World War II it was the state film company for the Nazi regime and in the Cold War it was the state film company for the Soviet supported GDR.

- **Sundance TV** is an American broadcast channel that operates as a premium subscription channel. Sundance TV commissions and purchases programming, sometimes investing in the production as part of a distribution deal. Sundance TV is owned by **AMC Networks**, a media conglomerate that broadcasts around the world. AMC bought Chellomedia, a cable network, allowing the channel to become global. AMC is a joint owner of **BBC America**.

- **RTL** is the largest private broadcaster in Germany. Its programmes are available free to viewers in Germany and surrounding European companies. It is a commercial television broadcaster, so much of its funding comes from advertising. RTL is also part of the RTL Group.

- **Freemantle Media International** is a television production and distribution company. It is owned by RTL, which is in turn owned by Bertelsmann – one of the largest media conglomerates in the world. It has divisions in Europe, Australia and America, and is engaged in producing and distributing programming globally. It owns several production companies (e.g. **TalkBack** and **Thames**) and produces programming ranging from scripted drama, reality TV and comedies to panel shows. It also owns a music company that creates theme tunes and incidental music. Its shows have been purchased for broadcast by many mainstream broadcasters around the world.

- **Channel 4** is a commercial broadcaster in the UK. It makes much of its money via advertising but also receives some public funding. It is a publisher-broadcaster and uses the 'Robin Hood system', where profitable programming is used to support programming that attracts smaller audiences and so would run at a loss. Channel 4 has to meet some specific broadcasting rules.

- **Walter Presents** is an area of the **All 4** streaming service, featuring television programmes from around the world. The programmes are selected by Walter Luzzolino, an Italian TV producer who provides a brief review by means of an introduction to each programme. The programmes on Walter Presents cover many different genres and represent programming from Asia, Europe and South America. The one thing they all share is that they are not in English. The programmes must all be popular in their own country, critically acclaimed or award-winning and must demonstrate a level of quality in their production values. Walter Presents also aims to show the best of mainstream rather than art house foreign-language productions.

Industry

ACTIVITY 4.27

Match the following terms to the correct definition.

Term	Definition
Commercial broadcaster	Where a media conglomerate owns companies that can deal with different stages of production.
Advertising	A large media corporation consisting of a collection of different media-related companies.
Conglomerate	A broadcaster that relies on advertising to generate an income
Vertical integration	A broadcaster that receives public money and hence has to provide some form of social and/or cultural service in return.
Public service broadcaster	Using profits from successful programming to help support less profitable shows.
Publisher-broadcaster	A promotional product attempting to promote or sell a product or service. The message is controlled by the person selling the product or service and they pay to get the message shown to the audience.
'Robin Hood' system of funding	The process by which small numbers of large companies control increasing proportions of media output.
Concentration of ownership	A broadcaster that commissions and buys programming but does not make it itself.

The industrial context of any media product impacts on the way it is **produced**, **distributed** and **circulated**.

Industrial context: production and distribution

ACTIVITY 4.28

Having looked at the industrial context of *Deutschland 83*, consider how you would respond to the following exam-style questions. You could:

a Make notes in the form of a plan for an answer to the questions.

b Construct a formal written answer to the following questions.

You should try to answer each question in 15–20 minutes.

1 What advantages are there for **production** companies that are part of a large media **conglomerate**?

2 How may Freemantle International's relationship with the RTL group have helped the global **distribution** of *Deutschland 1983*?

3 Why might having investment from both American and German producers be an advantage in getting **global distribution** for the product?

4 Why are some people concerned at the amount of power held by massive global **conglomerates** such as Disney and Bertelsmann?

Distribution

Channel 4's role is to **distribute** the programming it purchases from production companies.

<table>
<tr><td>Make a list of the different ways you could access Channel 4's programming</td><td>How have recent technological developments changed the way audiences access television content?</td></tr>
<tr><td></td><td></td></tr>
</table>

Explore the All 4 website.

1 Do you think the streaming service makes it easy for audiences to find programmes?

2 How is watching programming on Netflix or Amazon different for audiences?

Channel 4

Read the extract on the right from the Channel 4 website summarising the channel's public service remit.

Why do you think Channel 4 decided to buy the rights to broadcast *Deutschland 83*? How does this programme fit in with its remit?

Statutory public service remit – 15 elements, including:

- Be innovative and distinctive
- Stimulate public debate on contemporary issues
- Reflect cultural diversity of the UK
- Champion alternative points of view
- Inspire change in people's lives
- Nurture new and existing talent

Source: 'What is Channel 4?', www.channel4.com/corporate/about-4/who-we-are/what-is-channel-4

Circulation

Once a television programme is ready for distribution, people need to be made aware of it in order to attract an audience. The producers, distributors and broadcasters are all involved in attempts to increase the circulation of the product – that is, encourage as many people as possible to watch the programme. This means there will be an advertising and marketing campaign to try help promote the programme.

 ACTIVITY 4.31 List the ways a media company can promote a television programme. Try to think of different ways that the three media platforms could be used.

Print	Broadcast	e-Media

Undertake some research online to find promotional material used to market *Deutschland 83*. You should look at print, broadcast and e-media materials.

All promotional material needs to raise awareness of the product, create interest and persuade the audience to act (watch the programme).

Broadcast marketing

 ACTIVITY 4.32 Watch the trailer for *Deutschland 83* on YouTube (www.youtube.com/watch?v=Eb0yFr2jVAU).

How is the media language in it used to raise awareness, create interest and persuade the audience to act?

The trailer raises awareness when it ...	The trailer uses the following to try to create interest in the programme ...	The techniques used to persuade the audience to want to watch the show are ...

Print marketing

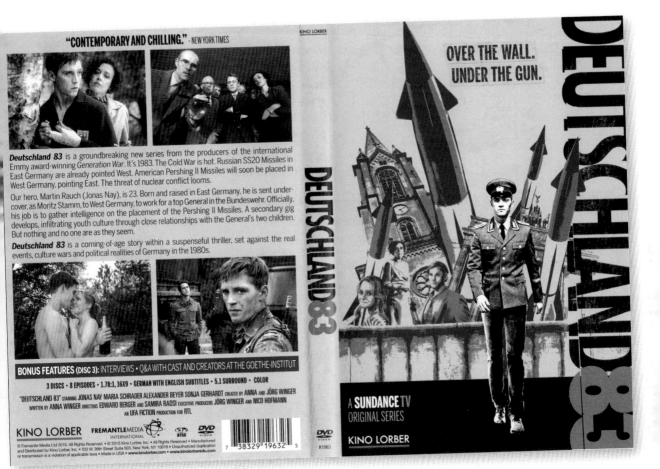

ACTIVITY 4.33

Show where the DVD cover for *Deutschland 83* (above) is trying to create audience interest and appeal in the following ways. There could be several examples of these techniques on the cover:

- By using the authoritative opinion of a respected reviewer.
- By offering the audience something different.
- By offering the audience a quality production.
- By offering the audience excitement.
- By creating an enigma about the programme.
- By offering the audience romance.
- By offering the audience tension and drama.
- By offering the audience nostalgia.

e-Media marketing

The *Deutschland 83* Facebook page has been redesigned to promote the second series, which is called *Deutschland 86*. Read through the posts made on the Facebook page , then answer the following questions.

1. How is the Facebook page used to encourage interaction with the audience?
2. How are the audience encouraged to share information about *Deutschland 83/86*?
3. What benefits does online marketing offer media producers?

e-Media distribution and marketing

Go online to the Walter Presents pages of the All 4 website.

Explore the other programmes that are distributed there.

Watch the introduction to *Deutschland 83* and identify the techniques used by Walter to sell the series.

How Walter uses persuasive language to describe the programme.	
How Walter uses genre to generate audience interest.	
How Walter uses other media products to help generate audience interest.	
How the selection of clips from the programme are used to create appeal.	
How Walter communicates the tone and style of the programme.	
What audience expectations are created by the introduction.	

Audience

Having looked at some of the advertising and marketing materials, how would you define the target audience for *Deutschland 83*?

Target audience

Define the audience using demographic and psychographic categories, taking the following into account:

- The fact it is broadcast on Channel 4.
- The way Walter Presents creates a specialised area for the audience.
- The fact the programme is not broadcast in English.
- The fact it is set in the 1980s.

Audience demographics

Audience psychographics

Deutschland 83 attracted 2.5 million viewers, thus becoming the most watched non-English-language drama in the history of British TV. It won a number of awards, including an International Emmy in 2016, and received very positive reviews around the world. It has a user rating of 8.2 out of 10 on IMDb.

Information for the audience

ACTIVITY
4.37

Access the Metacritic page (www.metacritic.com/tv/deutschland-83) to read some professional reviews of *Deutschland 83*. For a UK response you can find lots of discussions on the programme in the *Guardian* (www.theguardian.com/tv-and-radio/deutschland-83).

1 What positive and or negative points are raised by professional reviewers?

2 Read some of the user comments on IMDb: www.imdb.com/title/tt4445154/?ref_=nv_sr_2. Summarise some of the reasons they like the series.

3 Summarise some of the negative comments about the series.

4 Why are other people's opinions an important factor in the success of a television programme?

5 Do you think professional reviewers are important?

6 Do you think the opinion of audience members can be influential?

Audience interpretation

Despite its global success, the first series of *Deutschland 83* was not a big hit in Germany.

Read Philip Oltermann's (2016, 17 February) analysis of the programme, 'Deutschland 83 has Wowed the World – Pity the Germans don't Like it', from the *Guardian* and answer the questions below. You will find the full article here: www.theguardian.com/commentisfree/2016/feb/17/deutschland-83-wowed-world-germans-dont-like-it.

Deutschland 83 has wowed the world – pity the Germans don't like it
Philip Oltermann

The radical premise of this cold war drama – engaging with East Germany's worldview – has won it many fans, but for Germany it still sends shivers

▲ 'Deutschland 83 was designed to be the big ballsy production that restored German TV's pride, with the marketing budget to go with it.' Photograph: Nik Konietzny/Channel 4

1 What happened to the viewing figures in Germany by the end of Series 1?

2 What reason does the writer offer to explain its fall in popularity?

Now apply some theory.

3 How can reception theory be used to explain the different response to the programme in Germany? For example, consider how the following may be interpreted differently by German and British audiences:

a The way the programme sets an agenda.

b The framing of the story.

c The use of myths that surround the idea of the 1980s and the Cold War era.

4 How might the nationality of the audience create a different **condition of consumption**?

5 How might the nationality of the audience influence the way the **encoded** messages are **decoded**?

6 How might the nationality of the audience member influence the creation of a:

   a **hegemonic** reception of the programme's ideas

   b **negotiated** reception of the programme's ideas

   c **oppositional** reception of the programme's ideas?

Even though it was received differently in Germany, the programme was considered a global success.

Audience gratifications

1 Why do you think *Deutschland 83* proved popular with a global audience?

   Use examples from the first episode to show how it may provide the following gratifications:

Gratification	Examples from the episode
Information/education	
Entertainment (try to find several different types of entertainment in the episode, e.g. excitement, nostalgia, escapism, tension)	
Social interaction	
Personal identity	

(Continued)

2 Which gratifications do you think are more important for the audience?

3 Which ones did the producers prioritise?

Summary: *Deutschland 83*

ACTIVITY
4.40

To summarise your work on *Deutschland 83*, discuss why you feel the programme was a success around the world.

- Use your knowledge of the industry context of the product to explain why it was able to be distributed widely and circulated successfully.
- Use your knowledge of audience theories and debates to discuss why it was able to attract and maintain an audience.

4.3 Targeted close study product 3: *Hidden Figures*

Media Form: Film

Targeted area of the theoretical framework: industry

BASED ON THE UNTOLD TRUE STORY
HIDDEN FIGURES

REVISION BOOSTER

Even though you are not being assessed on your knowledge of the film, you will need to be able to provide detailed examples in the exam. For this CSP, examples will come from the information you uncover about the industrial context of the film.

TIP Don't forget, *Hidden Figures* is to be studied as an industry case study. You do not have to watch the film (but of course you can) and you will not be assessed on your knowledge of the film itself.

ACTIVITY 4.41

Identify the form and function of *Hidden Figures.*

1 **Media form?**
   a Film
   b Advertising and marketing
   c Television

2 **Method of production?**
   a Audio
   b Moving image
   c Print

3 **Method of distribution?**
   a Television   c Online
   b Cinema   d Radio

4 **What is the main function of this product?**
   a To provide information.
   b To entertain the audience.
   c To persuade the audience to do something.
   d To create a personal communication with the audience.

Facts and figures

ACTIVITY 4.42

What do you know about the film *Hidden Figures*?

What year was it released?	
Who is the director?	
What is the film about and what is the source of the story?	
What is historically significant about the story?	

There are three industrial processes that can help structure your revision for this CSP:

- **Production:** the making of the film
- **Distribution:** getting the film to the audience
- **Circulation:** getting the audience to the film

Production: the making of the film

The production companies involved in making *Hidden Figures* were Fox 2000 Pictures, Chemin Entertainment and Levantine Films. Production companies are involved in the financing of films. Large production companies are often involved; Fox 2000 Pictures is a subsidiary of 20th Century Fox, which in turn is part of a much bigger media company.

REVISION BOOSTER

Factual information about the industrial context of films can be found online. Some good sources are:

- imdb.com
- wikipedia.org
- boxofficemojo.com.

Industrial context

What can you find out about **Fox 2000 Pictures/20th Century Fox**?

1 Who was it owned by when *Hidden Figures* was made? Who owns it now?

2 What other companies are part of this media conglomerate?

3 What other types of things does Fox do other than film production?

4 How could having a big Hollywood conglomerate help in the production of a relatively low-budget film?

5 What can you find out about Chemin Entertainment and Levantine Films?

6 What connections can you make between Chemin Entertainment and Fox 2000 Pictures?

(Continued)

7   What kind of media products has Chemin Entertainment supported in the past?

8   How does Levantine Films define its unique brand identity?

Levantine Films makes character driven, artistically ambitious and socially relevant films. We are interested in linking history, and counter-history, with the present, celebrating unrecognised heroes, and affecting social impact. We aim to promote understanding and inspire dialogue across cultures, while challenging stereotypes through the power of great storytelling.

Source: www.levantine-films.com

9   How could each of these companies offer different benefits in the production of *Hidden Figures*?

Fox 2000 Pictures	Chemin Entertainment	Levantine Films

Hidden Figures was produced on a budget of $25 million. This is a much smaller production budget than, for example, *Black Panther*, which had over $200 million to spend on production.

Production budgets impact on the way a film is produced in many different ways.

The financial context of production

ACTIVITY 4.44

How would this budget have impacted on the way the film was produced? Consider the following.

Media language choices	Casting	The genre of the film	The way the story is told

Economic risk

ACTIVITY 4.45

1 Medium-budget films such as this are often seen as a good investment. Why is this?

2 In what ways could *Hidden Figures* have been a risky investment?

REVISION BOOSTER

As you don't have to watch the film, you could find examples of media language choices and the way genre and narrative codes are used in trailers and other promotional material.

Distribution: getting the film to the audience

Hidden Figures had quite a traditional initial distribution for a medium-budget film, being distributed by 20th Century Fox. It was initially given a limited release on Christmas Day in 2016 but then had a general release and it was played in lots of cinemas in the USA. The film was later released in Canada, parts of Europe and South America before being released in the UK in February 2017 and then all around the world in February and March of that year. It wasn't released in Japan, though, until September 2017.

Financial success

ACTIVITY 4.46

1 How much money did the film make at the box office in the USA?

2 How much money did the film make at the box office around the world?

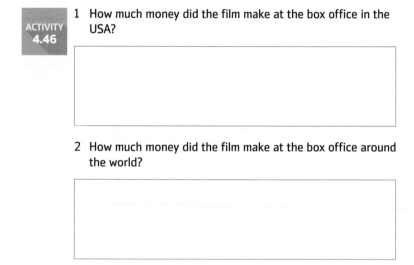

Distribution

Compared with big-budget films such as *Black Panther* (which has made over $1.3 billion), *Hidden Figures'* profits seem quite small but, because it only had a small production budget, the film can be seen as a success. It made almost ten times its budget in box office takings.

Black Panther made over $1.3 billion.

Having a wide distribution enables audiences to see the film easily. Once a film stops being shown at the cinema, the distribution company can use other methods to make the film available to watch.

ACTIVITY 4.47

List the ways that *Hidden Figures* was distributed to audiences, other than being made available at the cinema.

Distribution methods

Circulation: getting the audience to the film

Just being shown in a cinema doesn't necessarily mean that the film will be a success. To make a profit the film has to be seen by audiences.

Advertising and marketing

Audiences who visit the cinema would have been made aware of *Hidden Figures* by the marketing taking place within the cinemas themselves but in order to get the film seen by as many people as possible, a range of advertising, marketing and promotional activities will be undertaken long before the film is released.

ACTIVITY 4.48	What types of advertising and marketing strategies are traditionally used when promoting a film?	How can films be marketed using digital and/or social media?

REVISION BOOSTER

You should be familiar with the specifics of the marketing materials created to promote *Hidden Figures* and use examples from posters, trailers, websites, social media and any other techniques to show how the studio tried to increase the film's circulation.

Evaluating strategies

The following are common methods used to promote films. Discuss how each method is used generally and what the benefits are of each method. Then identify the way *Hidden Figures* used them.

	Discuss the method and its benefits	*Hidden Figures*
Posters		
Teaser trailers		
Trailers		
Official website		
Social media (Facebook; Instagram; Twitter; YouTube, etc.)		
Internal cross-promotion (related media products, e.g. soundtrack album)		
Appearance at film festivals		
External cross-promotion (other companies and organisations)		
Merchandise		
Promotional tours and appearances (actors and crew)		
Special screenings		
Awards nominations		
Other		

Poster analysis

**ACTIVITY
4.50**

Create a close analysis of this *Hidden Figures* poster:
- Consider the way media language has been selected and combined.
- Consider how the poster attempts to appeal to the audience.

The poster for the film's UK release.

Advertising and marketing do not stop once the film is no longer playing at the cinema. The film will be promoted in the hope of reaching wider audiences when it is available via other distribution methods such as DVDs or the availability of the film on streaming services.

Context

The film had the potential to attract a broad audience. It is a film about black women but this does not define the appeal of the film. Historical, true story dramas are often very popular, especially when connected to stories related to big achievements such as NASA developing space travel.

The basic story of the film is communicated through the marketing materials. The story deals with the way black women's contribution to an important historical moment had been previously hidden. The film deals with a period in history when racism and sexism were commonplace. Black women had to deal with both.

The cast of *Hidden Figures* at the Screen Actors Guild Awards ceremony.

ACTIVITY 4.51

1   How can this story, set in 1961, be seen to be relevant for modern audiences?

2   Consider (or look up) the following hashtags and identify how they may relate to the story being told in the film.

#OscarsSoWhite	#BlackLivesMatter	#EverydaySexism	#MeToo

Summary: *Hidden Figures*

ACTIVITY 4.52

To summarise your work on *Hidden Figures*, consider the industrial context of the film to help explain why it became a success. Consider the way the film was produced, distributed and circulated to help support your explanations:

- Include facts about the industrial context of the film.
- Include examples from some of the marketing materials to support your points.

Introduction to in depth close study products

In depth CSPs need to be studied using all areas of the theoretical framework. You will be asked to show your knowledge of in depth CSPs in Section C of the AS examination.

5.1 In depth close study product 1: the *i*

Media form: Newspapers

TIP The exam board provides specific pages from the newspaper CSP in the CSP guidance booklet. It is possible that the pages will be updated, so you must make sure you have checked that you are looking at the current pages chosen by the exam board.

REVISION BOOSTER

Some of the revision activities here will refer to the pages selected for the 2019 examination taken from the 26 September 2017 edition of the *i* newspaper.

This revision guide will help you practise using the theoretical framework and offer ideas as to how you can apply these ideas to the newspaper. You must ensure that you discuss the current selected pages to provide examples in the examination.

Introduction to the CSP

The *i* is a British daily newspaper. It is a relatively new title and was launched as a tabloid-sized, quality newspaper as a 'sister paper' for the broadsheet, the *Independent*. The *Independent* subsequently stopped being published as a print newspaper and is now available only as an online news source. The *i* newspaper has a daily print edition as well as a website.

The logo for the *i* newspaper

Industry

Your study of media industries has two elements. You will need to know some **facts** about the industrial context of the CSPs and you will also need to consider the **relevant industrial ideas** from the theoretical framework and apply them to the CSP.

Some facts and figures

ACTIVITY 5.1

Collect together some information about the newspaper. If you do not have this information in your class notes, you could go to the websites below where you will find the answers to the questions in the table:

- Wikipedia, 'i (Newspaper)', https://en.wikipedia.org/wiki/I_(newspaper).
- Newsworks, 'Discover the effectiveness of newsbrands: i', www.newsworks.org.uk/i.
- Wikipedia, 'JPIMedia', https://en.wikipedia.org/wiki/JPIMedia.
- www.jpimedia.co.uk/.
- Wikipedia, 'List of Newspapers in the United Kingdom by Circulation', https://en.wikipedia.org/wiki/List_of_newspapers_in_the_United_Kingdom_by_circulation.
- Statista, 'Circulation of Newspapers in the United Kingdom (UK) as of June 2018 (in 1,000 Copies)', www.statista.com/statistics/529060/uk-newspaper-market-by-circulation/.
- Freddy Mayhew (2018, 29 August) 'The i Newspaper Made £6m in First Half of 2018 Helping Offset Revenue Decline Across Publisher Johnston Press', *Press Gazette*, www.pressgazette.co.uk/the-i-newspaper-made-6m-in-first-half-of-2018-helping-offset-wider-revenue-decline-across-publisher-johnston-press/.

1 When was the *i* newspaper launched?		9 What can you find out about the current publisher?	
2 What was the name of the *i* newspaper's sister paper?		10 What is the *i* newspaper's circulation as of 2018?	
3 What was the difference between the two papers?		11 How does this compare with other UK newspapers' circulation figures?	
4 What happened to the sister paper in March 2016?		12 What is the *i* newspaper's current financial position?	
5 Define the *i* newspaper's unique brand identity.		13 Who is the current editor of the *i* newspaper?	
6 Who owned the newspaper from 2010 to 2016?		14 How much does a copy of the *i* cost to buy?	
7 What company published the *i* newspaper from February 2016?		15 What is the name of the organisation that regulates the newspaper industry?	
8 What happened to the publishing company in November 2018?			

Titles that are published by jpi media include:

i	The Extra	Times	Cumbernauld News
The Scotsman	Hebden Bridge Times	Belper News	Derry Journal
Yorkshire Post	Brighouse Echo	Batley & Birstall News	Dewsbury Reporter
Evening Post	Tyrone Times	Ballymena Times	Dromore Leader
Sunderland	Filey & Hunmanby	Bedford Today	Diss Express
Edinburgh News	Bainbridge Leader	The Local	Farming Life
Derbyshire Times	Berwick Advertiser	Brighton & Hove	Ellon Times
The Star	Ballymoney Times	Independent	Fife Today
Carrick Times	Arbroath Herald	Boston Standard	Harrogate Advertiser
Hayling Islander	The Gazette	The Berwickshire	Frasburgh Herald
News Letter	West Sussex Today	Chichester Observer	Dispatch
Sussex Express	Wetherby News	Bury Free Press	Horncastle News
Weston Advertiser	Tring Today	The Buteman	Hemel Today
Hawick News	Stornoway Gazette	Chad	Hartlepool Mail
Skegness Standard	Falkirk Herald	Daventry Express	Ulster Star
Forfar Dispatch	Barnoldswick & Earby	Coleraine Times	Ripon Gazette

Having this factual information about the *i* newspaper is important, but to prepare for the examination you will need to be able to link the newspaper's industrial context to issues and debates about media industries. This information will also be a useful background to your analysis of the newspaper using other areas of the theoretical framework. These 'industry' activities will draw in ideas from all areas of the framework. As with other CSPs, it is often helpful to consider industry issues by thinking about the specific issues the media product has to deal with in terms of:

- production
- distribution and
- circulation.

Production

The *i* is a daily, national newspaper. It has an online presence but it publishes a print edition every day. It was launched in 2010.

The impact of technology

ACTIVITY 5.2

What technological changes had been happening in the newspaper industry since the start of the 21st century? Look at the following list of just some of the recent technological developments and consider how they may have changed the way newspapers are produced:

a 24-hour rolling news (TV)

b multi-channel TV

c the internet

d broadband

e video/audio streaming

f smartphones and tablets

g 3G/4G

h Google's search engine

i Facebook

j Twitter

k YouTube

l news aggregators such as *Huff Post*

m online news sources such as *TMZ*.

Distribution

Traditionally, audiences bought a hard copy newspaper in the morning and it summarised 'yesterday's' news events. Newspapers were printed in black and white until technological advances made colour printing cheaper and easier (the first colour newspaper in the UK was *Today*, first published in 1986).

News sources

ACTIVITY 5.3

How might audiences access news today? Try to identify as many different sources of news for modern audiences by completing the following tables.

1   What gratifications do these sources of news offer audiences?

Modern source of news	Audience gratifications
Twitter	Short and instantly updated.
24-hour rolling news (TV)	Instantly updated. Audience can 'dip in' at any time of day to receive updates.

2   Are there any negative sides to these new and modern ways to get the news? Think critically and see if you can identify any problems they may raise.

Modern source of news	Possible issues
Twitter	Not always accurate.
24-hour rolling news (TV)	Often speculates when filling time.

The cost of distributing news in print form is much higher than using digital technologies. Print newspapers use paper and ink, and have to be transported to locations such as supermarkets and newsagents. These costs need to be recouped and print newspapers rely on audiences paying a cover price. The number of readers also impacts on how much they can charge for advertising space – the larger the audience, the more income the newspaper will make. Not only do audiences prefer the accessibility, immediacy and variety offered by digital news sources, they also like the fact that the information is often free. Online news sources have fewer costs to meet to get their news to the audience. They sell audience data to marketing companies and this is what funds online news reporting.

Circulation

As online and mobile technology has developed, print-based newspapers found they have been struggling with their circulation. Newspaper sales have declined dramatically since the start of the 21st century. The decline in circulation means that newspapers are losing out on sales revenue, but it also means that they have suffered a decline in income from advertising sales.

Making a profit

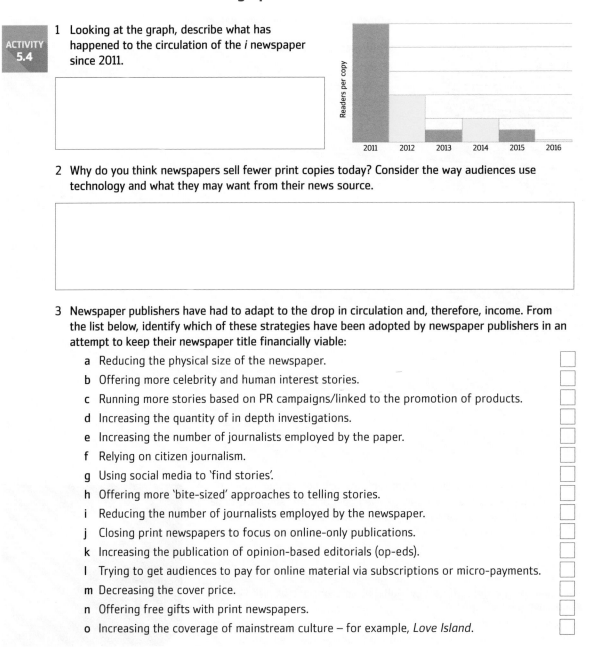

ACTIVITY 5.4

1 Looking at the graph, describe what has happened to the circulation of the *i* newspaper since 2011.

2 Why do you think newspapers sell fewer print copies today? Consider the way audiences use technology and what they may want from their news source.

3 Newspaper publishers have had to adapt to the drop in circulation and, therefore, income. From the list below, identify which of these strategies have been adopted by newspaper publishers in an attempt to keep their newspaper title financially viable:

   a Reducing the physical size of the newspaper. ☐

   b Offering more celebrity and human interest stories. ☐

   c Running more stories based on PR campaigns/linked to the promotion of products. ☐

   d Increasing the quantity of in depth investigations. ☐

   e Increasing the number of journalists employed by the paper. ☐

   f Relying on citizen journalism. ☐

   g Using social media to 'find stories'. ☐

   h Offering more 'bite-sized' approaches to telling stories. ☐

   i Reducing the number of journalists employed by the newspaper. ☐

   j Closing print newspapers to focus on online-only publications. ☐

   k Increasing the publication of opinion-based editorials (op-eds). ☐

   l Trying to get audiences to pay for online material via subscriptions or micro-payments. ☐

   m Decreasing the cover price. ☐

   n Offering free gifts with print newspapers. ☐

   o Increasing the coverage of mainstream culture – for example, *Love Island*. ☐

As we have seen, the current technological and economic context of the newspaper industry is impacting on the way newspapers are produced, distributed and circulated. These issues will be addressed as these ideas are applied specifically to the *i*.

Media language – genre

British newspapers have traditionally been categorised into two main genres: **broadsheet** or **tabloid**. Once, these terms referred to the size of the paper the newspapers were printed on. Today, though, these terms refer to the style of reporting and the news values of the individual titles.

Traditional broadsheet and tabloid front pages both in terms of design and style of reporting

	Style of reporting	News values
Broadsheet	Serious, factual tone; detailed analysis of events; discussion on the social impact of events.	Prioritises information over entertainment; offers more hard news; seeks to explain, analyse and offer its readers multiple perspectives. Will have a political agenda.
Tabloid	Emotional, sensationalist tone; limited explanation and detail offered on the cause of events – reports just on the event itself; engagement with the personal elements of a story.	Prioritises entertainment over information; offers more soft news; seeks to create emotional response in its audience; often only provides one single point of view; has an explicit political agenda.

Genre

1 How would you define the genre of the *i*? Does it use broadsheet conventions, tabloid conventions or both? Provide examples from your CSP pages to support your ideas.

Examples of broadsheet conventions used by the *i*	Examples of tabloid conventions used by the *i*

2 What is the term used to describe a media product that uses codes and conventions from more than one genre?

3 Neale says that genres need to adapt over time if they are to survive. How does your analysis of the *i* newspaper support this idea?

4 What economic advantage might the *i* newspaper gain if it uses both tabloid and broadsheet conventions?

Media language – layout and design

Newspaper conventions

Print-based newspapers share some common layout and design conventions. These conventions make newspapers recognisable and distinct from other print products such as magazines and advertising.

ACTIVITY 5.6 List the media language choices made in the production of your CSP pages that identify it as a newspaper. Add a brief description to show how the *i* uses these newspaper codes and try to add some more codes yourself.

Media language choices – newspaper codes	How they are used in the *i* newspaper
Use of front page headline	
Use of a main front page image	
Use of newspaper title and tagline	
Use of illustrative images	
Use of columns	
Use of headings and subheadings	
Type of language used in headlines	
Type of language used in articles	

Media language – selection and combination

Newspaper editors will select which stories they want to put in their newspaper. Every day there are hundreds of events but very few of them make it into the newspapers, so the stories that are chosen must be seen to be significant to the editor of the newspaper. The editor will also show how important a story is by its placement in the newspaper and the amount of space it is given in both words and images.

Meaning is created by the combination of page design, words and images. Individual media language choices are selected for the meaning they communicate to the audience and the way they create the newspaper's **intended meaning**. The process of **signification** comes from the media language choices that create **connotations** and act together via **anchorage**. **Symbolism** can be used in an attempt to **position** the audience into making a **preferred reading**. Stories can be related to specific **ideologies** and/or cultural **myths**.

Semiotics

Using the pages from your newspaper CSP, identify how media language choices create meaning. To do this:

- Consider how the layout and design of the newspaper are used to create meaning.
- Consider how the words and images have been selected and arranged to create meaning.
- Consider specific media language choices to show how they relate to the following terms and ideas:

• connotations	• ideology	• intended meaning
• symbols	• anchorage	• preferred meaning.

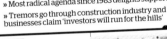

The 2019 newspaper CSP

An example

In the 26 September edition of the newspaper, a speech made by the Labour deputy leader is given significance by making it the **front page story** and then continuing the discussion on the points raised inside the newspaper. The **headline** on the front page uses a **large font** to highlight one of the main points of the speech. It is made more dominant by the use of **white text** on **black boxes** on the mainly **white page**. Further points from the speech are summarised in **bullet points** and a **small image** of John McDonnell is used on the **right of the front page**. The **relative size** of the image compared with the **headline** and detail from the speech acts as a **symbol**, creating an **intended meaning** that the **words are more important** than the personality of the speaker. The language used in the bullet points includes the phrase 'hundreds of billions' and the words 'radical' and 'tremors', which could create **negative connotations** and lead the audience towards a **critical interpretation** of the ideas from the speech. Supporters of McDonnell are said to be 'delighted' but, as they are defined as a specific group, this creates **connotations** of **otherness**. The **front page** appears to be **factual** in tone as would be expected in a **broadsheet**, but the focus on the speech's content and the language used could indicate that the *i* is taking a slightly critical approach to the politician's plans. The **front page** does not openly criticise the ideas and so the paper avoids constructing a **specific ideology** and this allows the **audience** to engage with the ideas and construct their own **interpretations**, but this may be led by the subtle negativity created in the language choices.

This approach to **reporting the story**, offering facts but with some language choices that create **negative connotations**, is repeated in the detailed discussion inside the newspaper. The **image dominates** this part of the CSP and shows two politicians in a **friendly pose**. Both men are wearing **red ties** and are shown against the **plain red backdrop** used at the Labour Party conference. Some audience members may make a **positive reading** of this image and the content of the article. The **symbolism** of the colour red in this **political context** is that it represents the political values of 'the left'. Some audience members will **interpret this negatively**. The final interpretation of the media language choices will depend on the audience member's own political sympathies and beliefs.

> **TIP** When discussing the *i* newspaper in the examination, always use the pages from your CSP to illustrate your response and offer detailed and specific examples from the pages you are given.

Media language – narrative

Another way to communicate meaning is to use narrative codes. It can be difficult to find narrative structures in print products as it is more usual to use these ideas when looking at media products that develop their stories over time.

Most news stories are based on a conflict – often the conflict will be centred on a binary opposition. In hard news stories these could include:

- Crime vs Law/the Police
- Conservative vs Labour
- UK vs Europe
- Leave vs Remain
- Peace vs War
- Right vs Wrong
- The prime minister vs The leader of the opposition party.

The political agenda of a news report can be identified by analysing the binary oppositions. One side of the opposition is usually presented more favourably and this indicates where the newspaper's political sympathies lie. Newspapers will usually make it clear what they feel the ideal solution to the problem is. This is an indicator of the newspaper's ideological position on the subject being reported on.

Narrative

ACTIVITY 5.8

Go through your newspaper CSP and identify binary oppositions.

When looking at the binaries, does one side of the opposition seem to be presented more favourably than the other?

If so, you may be beginning to identify the newspaper's own political agenda.

In narrative theory, conflicts define the nature of disequilibrium (Todorov), so analysing the binaries should give an indication of what the equilibrium was before the disruption and the ideological values presented in the conflict may indicate what the new equilibrium should be.

1. Using some of the disruptions/conflicts created by the binary oppositions identified above. Can you identify the equilibrium and/or the new equilibrium related to each conflict?
2. Does the newspaper offer its own ideal new equilibrium? This will reflect its ideological position.

	Equilibrium	Conflict/disequilibrium	New equilibrium
27 September 2017 'Analysis'	The world before the Brexit referendum.	The political divide over approaches to Brexit with a focus on the Labour Party.	The resolution of the division – political consensus.

Newspapers often use narrative roles (Propp) to tell their stories.

3 Can you see any of the following roles (or any others) being used in your newspaper CSP?

Narrative role	Example from the CSP
Hero	
Villain	
Princess	
Helper/donor	

Media representations

Representations are created when media language is **selected, combined and organised**, as shown earlier.

Sterotypes

Media producers often use **stereotypes** in the way they represent people, groups, places and ideas. Stereotypes are often based on ideas that have, over time, become the **constructed reality** about a group or place. Stereotypes often represent **hegemonic ideas** about the subject that reflect the producing culture's **dominant ideologies**. Stereotypes can be built on ideas about how a group looks or ideas about its attitudes and behaviours.

Commonly stereotyped groups

1 If a mainstream newspaper was to represent the following, what stereotypes might they use?

Subject of representation	Common appearance-based stereotypes	Common behaviour-/attitude-based stereotypes
Teenagers		
Students		
Pensioners		
Star Wars fans		
Football fans		
Conservative politicians		
Labour politicians		
People who live in cities		
People who live in the countryside		

2 Why do media producers often rely on stereotypes?

3 Why might the repeated use of stereotypes be problematic?

Some media products consciously try to avoid stereotypical representations. They may try to actively represent a group in ways that **subvert** the conventional ways they are represented. They may try to correct previous **misrepresentations**, create **countertypes** or deliberately try to create representations of groups or places that are usually **under-represented**.

Subverting stereotypes?

ACTIVITY
5.10

1 Define these terms.

Term	Definition
Stereotype	
Countertype	
Misrepresented	
Under-represented	

2 Look through the pages of your newspaper CSP again and answer the following questions.

What **stereotypes** are being used?	
Identify how media language is used to construct the **stereotypes**?	
Do you feel the **stereotypes** are in any way accurate?	
Do you see any evidence that the newspaper is trying to avoid **using stereotypes** or, perhaps deliberately trying to **subvert** them by using **countertypes**? If so, identify how this is done.	
Do you see any evidence for the newspaper representing **under-represented** groups or correcting **misrepresentations**? If so, identify how this is done.	

Stereotypes can be used to communicate the newspaper's agenda. **Positive representations** can **position the audience** to feel more sympathetic towards the subject of the representation and negative representations less so. **Negative representations** can be used to support attacks on the group and may reinforce the idea that some groups are outside the dominant culture – are 'other'. Negative representations encourage the audience to see the ideas being represented as wrong or invalid in some way.

ACTIVITY 5.11

1 Are there examples of negative stereotypes in your newspaper CSP?

If so, how is media language used to create these negative ideas about the subject?

2 Do you think the newspaper is using stereotypes to put its own political agenda forward?

If so, how has this been done?

3 Do you think that the audience are able to **decode** stereotypes differently and challenge the **intended meaning** communicated by the media producer?

If so, use the CSP to demonstrate how this could take place.

Audience – target audience

All newspapers have to consider who their target audience is. This allows them to **select** and **present** stories in ways that are most likely to **appeal** to the audience, offer them the **gratifications** they want and encourage them to buy the newspaper again.

One way to define target audiences is by **demographics**. YouGov (www.YouGov.co.uk) offers statistical information about brands and their target audiences. Here is the information on the age and gender of the readers of the *i* newspaper.

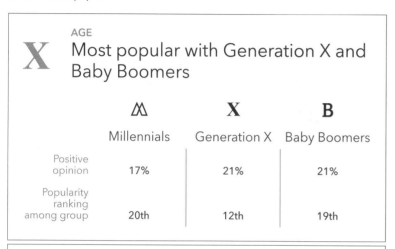

AGE **X** Most popular with Generation X and Baby Boomers			
	ᐃᐃ Millennials	**X** Generation X	**B** Baby Boomers
Positive opinion	17%	21%	21%
Popularity ranking among group	20th	12th	19th

GENDER **♂** Slightly more popular with Men		
	♀ Women	**♂** Men
Positive opinion	19%	21%
Popularity ranking among group	19th	13th

YouGov demographic data

Dividing the audience in this way doesn't offer much information though. We learn that fewer millennials read the paper than older readers, and that the paper is liked almost equally by men and women.

The *i* newspaper calls itself 'Britain's first and only concise quality title', so it might be more useful to think about the **psychographics** of the target audience. What type of personality would appreciate the *i* newspaper's approach to reporting the news? What gratifications does an *i* reader look for when reading a newspaper? What lifestyle priorities might they have? It would also be worth considering why someone would want to buy a physical newspaper when news is available free online.

1 As the *i* is a tabloid-sized daily newspaper that offers hard news presented in a brief format, describe the type of person that might be part of the newspaper's target audience.

2 Consider why someone may want to buy a newspaper rather than simply read one online. What advantages does the print newspaper offer its audience?

3 Looking at the stories selected by the editor in your CSP and the way the stories are presented, what **gratifications** (Blumler and Katz) might the *i* offer its readers?

When the *i* first launched, the publisher made these statements about their target audience:

'*i* is specifically targeted at readers and lapsed readers of quality newspapers and those of all ages,' the publisher said. '*i* will combine intelligence with brevity and depth with speed of reading, providing an essential daily briefing.'

'Ever since the *Independent* launched the paper has had a reputation for innovation and boldness and now we are creating the first postmodern newspaper, attractive to those who prize intelligence, convenience and desirability.'

'Time-poor newspaper readers, and especially commuters, have been telling us for years that they are inundated with information and just don't have the time to read a quality newspaper on a regular basis.'

Source: Mark Sweney (2019, 18 October) 'Independent's New Daily *i* to Target "Lapsed Readers of Quality Papers"', the *Guardian*, www.theguardian.com/media/2010/oct/18/independent-new-newspaper-i

Audience appeal

ACTIVITY
5.13

1 Using your CSP, identify how the paper can be shown to still be trying to meet the needs of the audience as defined on page 114 by the publisher.

2 Again, using examples from the CSP, in what ways do you think the paper is trying to respond to the technological changes and the competition from online news sources?

3 Identify media language choices and representations that are actively trying to create audience appeal.

Audience expectations and behaviours

Modern newspapers are fighting to survive as they are threatened by changes in audience expectations and behaviours.

ACTIVITY 5.14

1 Here is the list of modern developments from Activity 5.2. This time consider the way each development has changed audience expectations and behaviours when it comes to finding and accessing the news.

Modern news industry developments	Changes in audience expectations and behaviours
24-hour rolling news (TV)	Audiences expect that news is available at all times.
Multi-channel TV	
The internet	
Broadband	
Video/audio streaming	
Smartphones and tablets	
3G/4G	Online news is accessible anywhere where the audience has a phone signal.
Google's search engine	
Facebook	Audiences can access stories based on their previous interests and the interests of their social circle. Audiences can share news stories with their social circle.
Twitter	
YouTube	
News aggregators such as *Huff Post*	
Online news sources such as *TMZ*	

2 The following are some terms that relate to modern audiences and news. Connect the term with the correct definition

Citizen journalism	A reporting style where the events are reported as they happen.
Click-bait	A reporting style that summarises often complex issues into short lists.
Crowd sourcing	The use of news content created by members of the public.
Sensationalism	The use of dramatic or controversial headlines to attract the audience.
Listicles	A reporting style that relies on creating an emotional response from the audiences.
Live-blogging	Requests from news sources to get information from members of the public.

3 Using the pages from your CSP, can you see any evidence that the newspaper is trying to meet modern audience needs?

Regulation

As businesses, newspaper companies are under a lot of pressure. They are competing for audiences with other newspapers as well as television and online news, and they need to make money if they are to survive. The behaviour of journalists and newspapers is regulated, as they are expected to be honest and reliable. The *i* and most UK newspapers are regulated by the organisation IPSO.

Go to www.ipso.co.uk and then answer the following questions.

1 What is IPSO and what does it do?

2 Follow the link to read about the 'Editors' Code'.
   List five things that are regulated within the 'Editors' Code':

   i. _____   iv. _____

   ii. _____   v. _____

   iii. _____

3. Do you think regulating newspapers in this way is a good idea? If so, why or why not?

Summary – the *i* newspaper

ACTIVITY
5.16

To summarise your work on the *i* newspaper you should discuss the way the newspaper is attempting to appeal to its audience in the context of recent technological changes:

- Use your knowledge of the newspaper to discuss the way it uses **media language** and **representations** to create meaning and communicate to its audience.

- Use your knowledge of the **industrial context** of the newspaper to discuss the way it attempts to appeal to modern **audiences**.

5.2 In depth close study product 2: *The War of the Worlds* (1938)

Media form: Radio

Introduction to the CSP

The War of the Worlds is a radio drama that was broadcast live to its listeners on 30 October 1938. You will need to listen to a recording of the original production. It is available online and you can find it on YouTube, 'Orson Welles - War of the Worlds - Radio Broadcast 1938 - Complete Broadcast' (www.youtube.com/watch?v=XsOK4ApWI4g).

The War of the Worlds is an in depth CSP, so you will need to study it using all four areas of the theoretical framework. You could be asked to discuss this CSP in Section C of the AS exam. As it is an old media product, you will also need to consider the context of its production to be able to discuss this CSP effectively.

ACTIVITY 5.17

1 Gather together some factual information about the CSP, including:

   a Who wrote the original story?

   b Who directed the radio broadcast?

   c When was the drama originally broadcast and what is the significance of the date?

   d Which radio station broadcast the drama?

   e What was the name of the series that the broadcast was part of?

2 Create a brief plot summary of the events of the story.

3 Find out some information about the career of the director, Orson Welles.

The producer, director and narrator of *The War of the Worlds*, Orson Welles, was 23 when this famous radio drama was broadcast.

TIP Always give examples to support the points you make in an exam. Discuss the CSPs using specific detail about the way they were constructed, using the correct terms for the media language choices that were made.

It is important that you are familiar with the way media language was used to present the story to the audience.

Media language

The War of the Worlds is a radio broadcast, so has limitations in the type of media language it can use to tell the story. As there are no visuals, the story has to be told using sound, so radio producers need to make programmes that communicate their ideas quickly and clearly in order that listeners can understand the information or stories being presented. Radio dramas need to use words and sounds to allow listeners to imagine the locations and situations in the story.

Radio media language

ACTIVITY 5.18 Complete the following list of the type of sound choices available to radio producers:

- Dialogue

- Acting/presentation style

- Diegetic sound

As radio dramas can only use sound to communicate to their audience, audio codes and conventions have developed in the way stories are told to engage the listener. For example, the sound of a creaking door hinge is often used to tell listeners someone has just entered or left a room. Sound effects become a shorthand to help the audience understand what is going on. However, as Neil observed, the repeated use of conventions soon becomes tired and predictable.

Foley artists record sound effects made by everyday found objects.

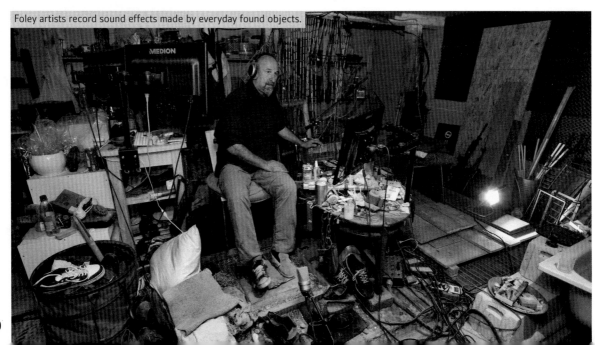

Semiotic analysis

ACTIVITY
5.19

1 Consider the following media language choices in the broadcast:

- interviewing experts
- the sound of a crowd
- the use of silence
- the role of the announcer
- the tone of the reporter's voice
- the sounds of the attacks
- the use of different locations (e.g. Grover's Mill, New Jersey and New York City).

Use some of the terms in the box below to help discuss how the media language choices above create meaning.

| connotations | symbol/symbolic | index/indexical | icon/iconic |

2 Discuss the way media language choices combine and work together to communicate meaning for the listener (anchorage).

Media language and genre

Radio drama producers often try to offer something new and unusual in the way they use sound. One way to achieve this is to experiment with the genre and narrative structure of the story.

Genre

The War of the Worlds is a science fiction story about alien invasion, but what genres and conventions of radio programming are used to tell the story in Welles' version? Describe the way the different genre codes are used.

Genre/radio conventions	Media language use
Drama	Introduction of the broadcast as being part of a 'Mercury Theatre' production. Voiceover creation of the exposition/equilibrium of the story.
Weather report	Announcer reading weather report.
Musical entertainment show	Announcer introduces a musical show. Presenter of show introduces the orchestra. The orchestra plays.

a Which of the following terms refers to a media product that uses codes and conventions of more than one genre?

b Which of the following terms refers to a media product that references other media forms or products?

	a	b			a	b
i. symbolism	☐	☐		iii. sub-genre	☐	☐
ii. hybrid	☐	☐		iv. intertextuality	☐	☐

The use of codes and conventions for different radio formats would have created **connotations** for the listening audience. Each media language choice is a **sign** that is used to **signify** meaning for the audience, and sound effects are used to **symbolise** specific ideas or events.

Media language and narrative

Radio dramas use narrative structures to tell their stories. Todorov's narrative structure can be applied to *The War of the Worlds*, as the drama begins with an equilibrium, then a conflict is introduced which creates disequilibrium that builds through the drama. The drama ends with a new equilibrium – the world survives but has been changed by the events of the drama.

Narrative

ACTIVITY
5.21

Using the narrative line below, apply Todorov's ideas to the way the story is developed in the radio broadcast.

1 How is the equilibrium established?

2 How is the problem introduced?

3 How does the problem develop?

4 What happens in the climactic moments of the disequilibrium?

5 Define the new equilibrium presented at the end of the broadcast.

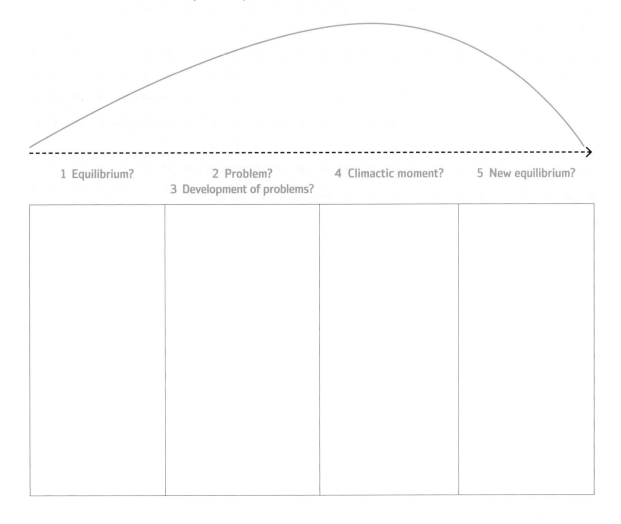

1 Equilibrium?   2 Problem?   4 Climactic moment?   5 New equilibrium?
                3 Development of problems?

Representations

 What ideas does *The War of the Worlds* create about the following groups represented in the broadcast?

	What ideas are created?	How are these ideas created (media language examples)?
Journalists and reporters		
Scientists/experts		
Politicians		
The general public		
The invaders		

It is clear that the director wished to create as **realistic** a **representation** of events as possible. In order to do this, the representations needed to relate to the context of production to ensure that audiences would find them believable.

The social context of production

 Consider these contextual issues. How may the events have influenced the representations created in the broadcast to make the drama more realistic?

Context of production	Influence on the representations in *The War of the Worlds*
The crash of the airship *Hindenburg* had been broadcast live on the radio in May 1937. The commentary from the radio broadcast can be heard on YouTube, '1937 Hindenburg Explosion in Colour with Herbert Morrison's Commentary' (www.youtube.com/watch?v=jH-mhZLuGRk). The video includes footage of the crash.	
The world was still suffering the effects of the Great Depression.	
Many European countries were experiencing political chaos and Europe was on the verge of World War II.	

The realism of the presentation and the social and political context of production could have had an influence on the way the broadcast was received. The representations reflect contemporary fears and concerns, so are likely to have resonated with the listening audience. Before we consider audience issues in more detail, it is worth thinking about the industrial context of the broadcast.

Industry/media context

ACTIVITY 5.24

1 Here are some facts about the industry/media context of *The War of the Worlds*. Which of these context issues have influenced the way the product was created?

2 Explain what the influence may have been.

The industrial context of production	How did the context influence production?	The influence may have been
Radio was a relatively new media form.		
News and entertainment had been provided by print media for many years but was now being challenged by film and radio.		
Radio was a direct challenge to print media as it was available in the audience's homes and offered immediate communication to a mass audience.		
The drama was broadcast by CBS (Columbia Broadcast System), a commercial radio broadcaster.		
CBS was one of two national broadcasters in the USA. They both competed for listeners.		
The Mercury Theatre on the Air series of radio dramas was under pressure to attract more listeners.		
Radio was regulated by the Federal Communication Commission.		

Audience – the context of reception

One of reasons why *The War of the Worlds* has become an important media product is due to the response to the programme. The drama was broadcast in a very different time when media experiences were collective rather than individual, as they tend to be now. Audiences in 1938 didn't have the number of choices for entertainment that modern audiences have. There were only four easily accessible media forms at the time: newspapers, magazines, films and radio. Audiences had access to print and radio in their own homes and by 1938 radio was the first true mass media form. There were only two radio broadcasters in the USA at that time, so most listeners would be listening to one or the other station. This created a shared culture as lots of people accessed the same radio programmes at the same time. The two radio broadcasters were competing for the audience's attention, as they both wanted the biggest share. Bigger audiences allowed the broadcaster to generate more advertising income.

Orson Welles broadcasting his famous adaptation of H. G. Welles' novel *The War of the Worlds*.

The broadcast of *The War of the Worlds* became infamous as it was blamed for creating panic in the listening audience. It was said that many audience members listening to the programme believed that aliens were attacking New Jersey and New York, and that their lives were in danger. The realism of the broadcast, and the fact that some audience members tuned in after the on-air announcement that the programme was a drama, meant that some people thought they were listening to an authentic report on events. Reports of panicked responses began during the broadcast and the next day newspapers were full of reports about people gathering to fight aliens. They also reported on stampedes, road accidents and losses of life being caused by attempts to escape the alien invasion.

CBS and Orson Welles were criticised for being irresponsible in presenting the story in the way they did and the **moral panic** that surrounded the broadcast was used to support the need for the regulation of the media based on an argument that it could have **negative effects** on audience members. In the days of mass media, these negative effects were thought to be able to impact on large groups of the population at the same time. The media (in this case radio) was thought to have the power to change the audience's attitudes and even their behaviour. Newspapers blamed radio and repeated concerns about its potential negative effect, reinforcing the idea that the **mass audience** was vulnerable and susceptible to being influenced by media messages.

Moral panic

Define the term, **moral panic**.

ACTIVITY
5.25

Mass audience effects theory

ACTIVITY 5.26

1 How does the reporting of the response to the drama support the following audience theories?

Bandura's ideas about the impact of violent media imagery	The hypodermic needle theory

2 Identify some of the criticisms used to challenge the viewpoint of these mass audience effects theories.

Criticisms of Bandura's ideas about the impact of violent media imagery	Criticisms of the hypodermic needle theory

The audience panic was widely reported in the newspapers at the time. The reports of the panic started in New York but spread across America and around the world, making *The War of the Worlds* one of the most famous radio programmes in history. The idea that it had created a mass response where people took to the streets to fight aliens or to flee the invasion became 'received knowledge' and was repeated in discussion and documentaries for decades after the event.

However, the evidence after the broadcast shows that there was no mass panic. Some listeners did phone in to CBS to complain that the drama was overly realistic, but some also phoned in to say how good it was.

The War of the Worlds myth

ACTIVITY
5.27

1 Watch the following commentary on YouTube about the facts of the response to the broadcast:
   • '*The War of the Worlds* Mass Panic (That Never Happened)' (www.youtube.com/watch?time_
     continue=17&v=7amqdrVO-E0).

2 Look at the following examples of reporting after the broadcast. What claims were made about the effects of the broadcast?

3 Consider the argument made by Campbell. He said, 'the so-called "panic broadcast" brought newspapers an exceptional opportunity to censure radio, a still-new medium that was becoming a serious competitor in providing news and advertising':

a Why would it have benefited newspapers to criticise this radio drama in the ways seen above?

(Continued)

b How have new media technologies been criticised in similar ways? Consider how moral panics have been created about the following media forms:

	Media form	Moral panic
Some music videos		
Horror films		
Gaming		
Social media		

Summary – *The War of the Worlds*

To summarise your work on *The War of the Worlds* you should discuss the impact of the context of production and reception. You will need to engage with the social context as well as the industry/ media context of a radio programme that was made and broadcast in 1938.

- Use your knowledge of the **media language** choices made in production to discuss the way the drama attempted to create a 'realistic' **representation** of the events of the story.
- Use your knowledge of the **context** of production to discuss the way the producers used contemporary fears and concerns to heighten the effects of the drama.
- Consider the way **audience engagement** was encouraged in the way it was produced.
- Use your knowledge of the **industrial context** of the radio drama to discuss the way the programme was responded to after its broadcast.
- Consider how the response to the drama reinforces some theories about the **effects of the media on audiences**.

Answers to activities

Introduction

This answer section offers definitions, examples and suggestions related to the activities in Chapters 1, 2 and 3.

It is important to be aware of the difference between 'fact' and 'interpretation'. The introduction to this revision guide discusses the need for knowledge of certain facts and definitions. Interpretations, though, should come from you and your application of this knowledge. This is why answers are not given for all activities, as some require a personal, analytical or interpretative response. In order to revise for your Media Studies exam, you need to practise your analysis skills and create your own interpretations of the CSPs.

For the same reason, there are no answers provided for Chapters 4 and 5 as the activities here are intended to help you generate ideas rather than provide them for you. The secret to success in Media Studies is your engagement with the ideas from the theoretical framework and practising applying these ideas to the CSPs.

Chapter 1 Media language

ACTIVITY 1.1

Media platform	Media language used	Examples of form	Specific media products
Print	Uses text and images only.	Newspapers	The *Daily Mail*, the *i*
Broadcast (audio)	Audio products use music, sound effects and the spoken word to communicate to audiences.	Music radio, News programmes, documentaries, drama, magazine shows	The Archers, Life Hacks, Newsbeat, Today, pm, breakfast/drive time shows, The Media Show
Broadcast (video)	Video products use images as well as sound. Video can use the spoken word as well as words on screen as required.	News bulletin, sit-com, crime drama, animation, game shows, reality TV, talk shows	The Good Place, No Offence, Rick and Morty, Strictly Come Dancing, The Graham Norton Show
e-Media	Can use still and moving imagery; can use audio consisting of sound, music and/or the spoken word; can use words in both short and long form.	Advertising website, online game, news site, lifestyle blog, online magazine	The Walkers Crisps site, Fortnite, The Guardian online, Goop, TeenVogue

a Close-up   b High-angle   c Long-shot   d Mid-shot

Title/masthead

Dateline/sell line

Cover model/star

Coverlines

Model identification/strapline

1

Definition	Term
The meaning or idea communicated by the use of a specific sign.	Signified
The image or sound used to communicate an idea.	Signified
An image or sound that is known to represent a specific object or idea but is not a literal representation of it.	Symbol

2 • **index** – where an image used has a logical connection to the idea being communicated, e.g. where an image of smoke is used to indicate fire

   • **ideology** – a system of belief/ways of thinking, e.g. the idea that we should have freedom of speech is ideological.

   • **myth** – the commonly held beliefs that are normalised through media representations: e.g. the continued connections made between women and housework normalising the idea that women are 'naturally' better at cleaning than men.

   • **dominant signifier** – the most commonly used signifiers that reflect culturally agreed meanings.

   • **anchorage** – the use of two or more media language elements to attempt to fix meaning and control audience interpretation.

3 • **paradigm and syntagm** – syntagm can be thought of as the 'rules' or conventions that limit choice and paradigmatic choices are made from the options that are available. For example, some syntagmatic options for a horror setting would be a cabin in the woods or a gothic mansion. Setting a horror series in a gothic mansion is a paradigmatic choice.

   • **denotation and connotation** – denotation is the literal meaning of a sign and connotations are the additional meanings created by the sign based on the associations created by the sign.

ACTIVITY 1.4

1 **Encoding** – the private jet, the watch, the gold tint/light flare, the confident body language, David Beckham.

2 **Encoding** – buying the watch will offer the consumer status as it is associated with a glamourous lifestyle.

3 **Decoding** – a negotiated reading may be a desire for the watch whilst rejecting the idea of wanting to buy into the lifestyle.

4 **Decoding** – the glamourous lifestyle reflects an elite and privileged position that is outside the reality of most people. It acts to normalise the view that wealth and luxury are ideals.

ACTIVITY 1.5

	Broadsheets	**Mid-market tabloids**	**Tabloids**
	The *Daily Telegraph*; the *Daily Guardian*; the *i*	The *Daily Express*; the *Daily Mail*	The *Daily Mirror*; the *Sun*
Appearance (layout and design)	Words dominate over images.	Offers more detailed information than red-top tabloids but less than broadsheets.	Images dominate over words.
News values (content)	Hard news dominates. Stories are analysed for their broad significance.	Hard news and soft news are reported. Soft news is often based on celebrity gossip. Hard news is often discussed in terms of its impact 'locally'.	Value soft news over hard news; often report on gossip, scandal and human interest stories.
Reporting style (lexis and tone)	Non-emotional, formal tone, tends to offer detail and explanations.	Often sensationalist, attempting to create an emotional response – often attempt to generate fear or anger.	Informal tone; simple lexis; often use puns and sensationalism.
General approach to newsworthy events	Often take a 'global' or big picture approach. How does the event impact on society/culture/the political landscape?	Often take a localised approach. How does the event impact on my life or the lives of my family?	Often take a personalised approach: how does this impact on me (or people like me)?

ACTIVITY 1.6

1 Government plans tax hike for high earners

2 Fat-cats hit by PM's tax plan

3 That's Rich! Wealthy will pay more

Media language	Sit-com	Crime drama
Use of camera	Multiple camera set up on 4th wall	Single camera set-ups, camera mobile and follows the action, drone shots used establish setting and tone
Use of lighting	High-key lighting	Lighting effects used to create atmosphere (including low-key lighting, colour effects, light flares, etc.)
Types of plot	Simple plots based on misunderstandings and/or relationship conflicts	Complex 'who-dunnit' plot with narrative twists and turns
Types of character	Simple stereotypes of characters – the dumb one, the neurotic one, etc.	Some stock characters (the detective with a dark past) but also complex characters with detailed psychological motivations

Requires a personal response.

Hybrid products offer multiple gratifications and help avoid the clichés created within each genre by creating something new and, possibly, unexpected.

Cowboys and 'Indians'	Gunfights
A saloon bar	A white-hatted sheriff
Piano music	A black-hatted villain
A homestead under threat	A desert-based frontier town setting

1   Answers for some are given below.

Genres of order	TV CSP	Genres of integration	TV CSP
The hero tends to be a lone individual – traditionally, the hero would be male.	*The Killing*: Sarah Lund has a partner but relies on her own interpretation of events and makes her own decisions. **Both:** The contested space is the safe, civilised society. It is under threat when a murderer is on the loose.	**The hero** is often a collective, a family, a couple or community. Female or feminine heroes may feature.	*No Offence*: The programme shows the importance of the investigative team.

(Continued)

Genres of order	TV CSP	Genres of integration	TV CSP
The setting is a contested space – a location that is being argued or fought over. The setting is ideologically unstable.	*Both: The threat to the community is violent.*	**The setting** is a civilised space that is largely ideologically stable. Settings are often communities or families.	
The conflict is often based on an externalised threat and is usually expressed through violence.	*Both: The murder must be 'eliminated' and removed from the community either by imprisonment or death.*	**The conflict** is internalised – the threat to the community comes from conflict between the members of the group and is expressed through emotion.	*No Offence: The investigative team are shown responding to each other emotionally – this can lead to small conflicts but the main conflict is external.*
The resolution will usually mean the elimination of the conflict, often via a literal or symbolic death.		**The resolution** will usually be in the form of an embrace, love or some form of unification.	*No Offence: Whilst its resolution is based on stopping the killer, the team are unified further in the solving of the case.*
Common themes include the hero taking on the problems and contradictions of the world they inhabit on behalf of others – protecting and saving those weaker than them. A 'macho' code of behaviour dominates. The hero is often isolated and self-reliant. The hero often doesn't benefit from the resolution – they may leave after saving the community or may die in the act of resolving the conflict. The hero is an individual who remains outside the community.	*The Killing: Sarah isoloates herself and prioritises her work over her family. She often personalises the investigation and can be seen to be mission based in her attempt to protect. Her approach means that she sacrifices her personal relationships for the greater good of society* *Both: Although the investigations often use force and violence – this is in response to threat rather than an ideological choice of violence.*	**Common themes** include those involved in the conflict becoming integrated into the wider community once their personal problems have been resolved. There is a maternal/familial code of behaviour that dominates the story. The resolution often shows the value of community, communication and cooperation.	*No Offence: Dinah is shown integrating the events of the crime into her personal life and this demonstrates a maternal code of behaviour.* *Viv is a maternal figure for those in her team and ideas of community, communication and co-operation are valued during the investigation.*

2   No answer supplied for this question.

	Genre of order/integration
TeenVogue.com	
The *i*	
Tomb Raider: Anniversary	The quest narrative of the game provides goals for the player to achieve via the avatar of Lara Croft. 'Villains' and physical challenges provided by the environment act to stand in the way of achieving the goals. The gameplay provides ways for the player to beat villains and overcome challenges, allowing them to progress closer to the goal.

1

	The Missing	*The Killing*	*Deutschland 83*
Equilibrium	The family (in the past) is shown to be happy. In the present they have had to come to terms with the fact their daughter Alice had gone missing.	Sarah is to be married and is moving house. Pernille and Theis are happily married.	Martin is shown to be leading a settled life with his family and his fiancée.
Disequilibrium	In the past, Alice goes missing, creating the initial disequilibrium. In the present, her return creates a secondary disequilibrium.	The episode begins with the attack on Nanna.	Martin is recruited to work undercover and is relocated to West Germany.
New equilibrium	The investigation of Alice's disappearance is reopened and linked to a previous kidnapping case.	By the end of the episode, Sarah is established as the lead investigator and is putting her private life on hold.	Martin is working as a spy.

2 No answer is given for this question.

No answer is given for this question.

Answers for some are given below.

Masterplot	Description	For example	CSP
Quest narrative	A story based on a journey based on a search for a person, place or thing.	*Requires a personal response.*	*The Missing*: based on the search for the truth about what happened to a missing child.
Revenge narrative	*A story based on the search for revenge for some sort of attack on the protagonist.*		
Transformation narrative	*A story based on the way an event or events cause a major change for one or more of the characters.*		*Men's Health*: the magazine helps the reader transform his body. *That Boss Life part 1* shows how Manny and Shayla's lives are transformed once they use the Maybelline mascara.
Discovery narrative	*A story based on a journey of discovery. This could be the discovery of something physical or it could be a personal discovery.*		
Maturation narrative	The 'coming of age story' – usually based around an event that takes the protagonist from being a child to becoming a young adult.		
Escape narrative	*A story based on the need to escape from a location. This could be a physical location (e.g. a prison) or the protagonist could be attempting to escape a situation.*		*Letter to the Free could be seen to be part of an 'escape narrative' where there is a need to escape the past and the institutionalised racism of US culture.*
Underdog narrative	A story based on someone fighting against adversity or some form of oppression.		*Hidden Figures*: shows how some black women battled racism and sexism to become successful in their profession.

Chapter 2 Media representations

ACTIVITY 2.1

No answer is given for this activity.

ACTIVITY 2.2

1

You are making a video news report about your home town. How would you create a positive representation using media language? Consider **what** you would show and **how** you would show it.	The news report (filmed on a sunny day) could focus on picturesque locations (e.g. beautiful buildings, parks, etc.). People would be shown in groups laughing and enjoying activities.
You are writing a film review for your blog-site. The film is called *Superheroes to the Rescue*. You didn't like the film. Create a headline that would represent the film negatively.	e.g. 'Someone Needs to Rescue these Superheroes'
You are directing a television drama and you want to show that your policeman protagonist is 'a man of mystery' with deep and possibly dark secrets. What media language choices would you make to create this representation? Also consider costume, location, props, lighting, camera work, acting direction, etc.	The detective could be dressed in black and grey clothing and, when in the busy and noisy police department offices, he could be positioned away from the team of police offers and shown to avoid small-talk and any personal conversations.
You need to select a picture of the Prime Minister that is going on the front page of the tabloid newspaper you edit, to accompany a story about a decision to create a new national bank holiday. The front page will be limited to the picture of the Prime Minister and a brief (but large) headline. Your newspaper supports the government's decision. Describe the type of image you would use and write a headline to represent the decision positively.	An image showing the Prime Minister in a position of power could be used to reinforce their authority (e.g. an image where the Prime Minister (at time of writing Theresa May) is in the centre of a group of members of the public where they are all looking at her and everyone is smiling broadly). Headline example: 'You May have the day off!'

2

You are making a video news report about your home town. How would you create a negative representation using media language? Consider **what** you would show and **how** you would show it.	The report should be filmed on a grey, overcast day and begin with a montage of images such as a litter strewn area, a polluted river and vandalised public areas.
You are writing a film review for your blog-site. The film is called *Superheroes to the Rescue*. You loved the film. Create a headline that would represent the film positively.	e.g. 'The new heroes of the superhero genre'
You are directing a television drama and you want to show that your policeman protagonist is a happy and upbeat person. What media language choices would you make to create this representation? Also consider costume, location, props, lighting, camera work, acting direction, etc.	The detective would be introduced walking into a surprise birthday party thrown by his friends and colleagues. In a party montage he would be shown dancing with his female boss and singing Karaoke with other detectives.

(Continued)

You need to select a picture of the Prime Minister that is going on the front page of the tabloid newspaper you edit, to accompany a story about a decision to create a new national bank holiday. The front page will be limited to the picture of the Prime Minister and a brief (but large) headline. Your newspaper does not support the government's decision. Describe the type of image you would use and write a headline to represent the decision negatively.	The image of the Prime Minister (at time of writing Theresa May) will be one where she is rushing past photographers with her collar up and her face partially hidden. She will look worried and harassed. Headline example: 'We need workers, not shirkers Mrs May'

ACTIVITY 2.3

The use of language in the headlines positions the audience to engage with the political agenda of each newspaper. For example, the *Mirror* and the *Guardian* both lead with an idea of looking for unity after the divisive Brexit vote, with the *Guardian* focusing on those who 'reach out' and the *Mirror* using the word 'reunite' placed over a symbolic image of a kiss featuring the flags of the EU and the UK. The *Times* reflects on how close the result was but the phrase 'close call' is used when a favoured result has been reached and the *Daily Express* is the most celebratory of all the newspapers, using a headline that is intended to position its audience to feel a sense of accomplishment, patriotism and sense of making history.

ACTIVITY 2.4

The male character in a Western is heroic.	A white hat	• Reading glasses and a roll-neck jumper
The female in a soap opera is the life and soul of the party.	Oversized jewellery and bright clothing	• A hoody and baseball cap
The female detective is an introvert.	Reading glasses and a roll-neck jumper	• A white hat
The young male in the drama cannot be trusted.	A hoody and baseball cap	• Oversized jewellery and bright clothing

ACTIVITY 2.5

1 An answer for one is given for one below.

CSP	Stereotypes
The Missing	
Deutschland 83	
Men's Health	Vin Diesel represents a traditional idea of masculinity. His pose in the photograph is constructed to show his muscular frame – especially his arms – and he represents an ideal of masculinity based on physical size and strength.
That Boss Life part 1	
Tomb Raider: Anniversary	

2 No answer is given for this question.

ACTIVITY 2.6

a This supports the hegemonic ideal that men are expected to be less emotionally expressive.

b This supports the dominant ideology of contemporary culture that wealth equates to success and value.

c This supports the ideology that is it sometimes necessary to seek professional excellence even if this means having to sacrifice other aspects of life.

d This supports the hegemonic ideal that men are expected to be physically strong.

e This supports the racist position that criminal behaviour is connected to ethnicity.

ACTIVITY 2.7

CSP analysis question.

ACTIVITY 2.8

CSP analysis question.

ACTIVITY 2.9

Masculine traits	Feminine traits
strong	emotional
loud	weak
unemotional	small
large	quiet
aggressive	passive
logical	intuitive
worker	nurturer
provider	domestic
active	still

ACTIVITY 2.10

CSP analysis question.

ACTIVITY 2.11

CSP analysis question.

ACTIVITY 2.12

No answer is given for this question.

ACTIVITY 3.1

Answers for some are given below.

Demographic group	Media product	How it attempts to please the target audience
Age	*Hollyoaks* (Channel 4)	It presents melodramatic storylines that often relate to youth culture, relationships and issues commonly associated with young people's life experiences.
Age		
Gender	www.glamourmagazine.co.uk	*Glamour* magazine targets females by presenting topics that are stereotypically of interest to women – fashion, beauty, celebrity gossip, etc.
Gender	www.gq-magazine.co.uk	GQ targets a male target audience by presenting topics stereotypically of interest to men. Fashion, sport, technology, etc. Also – see below
Gender		
Social class/ wealth	www.gq-magazine.co.uk	*GQ* magazine targets 'young professionals', promoting a lifestyle that values sophisticated fashion with some luxurious elements.
Social class/ wealth	www.glamourmagazine.co.uk	Glamour magazine reflects an aspirational lifestyle, focusing on fashion and lifestyle choices that connote success and status.
Social class/ wealth		

ACTIVITY 3.2

No answer is given for this activity.

ACTIVITY 3.3

Production	Distribution	Circulation
Production choices should be made considering the interests and desires of the target audience. Media language choices will always attempt to appeal to the stated target audience of the product.	It is important for producers to know what the habits and behaviours of the target audience are to ensure that the product is distributed in a way that will appeal to them. Lifestyle content should be offered online if the target audience spends most of their time on tablets/smartphones.	Similar to distribution, the behaviours of the target audience will help when making decisions that attempt to increase circulation. Knowing where the target audience are located (online, watching TV, etc.) will make it easier to find them so that there is a better chance that advertising and marketing will be seen by the people who may be interested in the product. Marketing methods will also need to be tailored for the target audience.

1

Term	Meaning	Techniques demonstrated in Activity 2.3 Newspapers
Agenda setting	Presenting information in such a way as to influence the perception of its importance.	The positioning of a story on a newspaper's front page indicates that it is perceived to be the most important story of the day. The Brexit vote dominates the front pages and this communicates its importance to the readers.
Framing	Presenting information with a specific focus on certain parts rather than presenting the whole story or a complete image. Framing can also take place by presenting information using a specific tone or with an identifiable attitude.	The *Daily Telegraph* presents the internal politics of the Conservative party as being the most important element of the story. This creates a narrow perspective but reflects the party loyalty that is central to the newspaper's political agenda.
Myth making	The repetition of or construction of popular ideas as if they are 'normal' or 'natural' when they represent a specific (and debatable) point of view.	The *Times* and the *Daily Express* both use images of Chelsea Pensioners on their front page. The image generates positive connotations about Britain's success in World War II and creates a nostalgic idea that is anchoring the response to the Brexit result. This plays on the myths of Britain's greatness and connoted a nostalgic idea of national identity.

2 The magazine's agenda is to encourage personal development and change. The coverlines focus on transformation narratives ('fun and laughter post-divorce') and offer examples and guidance for the audience to make changes in their own lives ('30 days to a creative life', 'Launch a second career'). The front cover is illustrated by an image of Drew Barrymore, who is a successful film and TV actress, famous for having a troubled youth but who is now presented as being a success in her personal and professional life. This anchors the agenda of transformation. Barrymore's happy and relaxed body language represents the ideal outcome of the magazine's agenda.

Conditions of consumption	Impact
Going to the cinema with a large friend group to watch a horror film.	Being in a cinema means that the film is the sole focus of attention. The room is dark and the screen and sound dominate. Being in a group may encourage a more visceral response to the horror. Some viewers may try to show how 'brave' they are when viewing horror with others.
Sitting at home alone watching a horror film on a tablet or computer.	The home environment may create distractions – other people, other media, other technologies, etc. Being alone may heighten the effect of the horror, as a lone audience member does not have the 'safety' that is provided by a group and the imagination of the viewer may add to the horror of the images on the screen.
Reading a newspaper at home alone.	This condition of consumption could allow the reader to focus on detail and engage with the complexities of a story.
Reading a news app on a noisy bus.	Being in public while trying to read can be distracting. It will be more difficult to engage with long-form writing and the details of a complex news event. Reading stories that are short and illustrated with lots of images may be a better option in this environment

Answers for two are given below.

Theory	Definition	Active and/ or passive	Arguments for and/or against this theory
Social learning theory (Bandura)	People imitate what they see.	Passive	The study was focused on very young children and so cannot be said to reflect how all people are likely to behave. The study did not test the effect of television or film imagery.
Hypodermic needle theory			
Uses and gratifications theory	Media audience choose what they want to access based on their own personal needs, desires and preferences	Active	This theory accepts that people act differently, avoiding the problem of assuming the audience is a single 'mass'. This theory also acknowledges that people make active choices for their own reasons.
Media literacy			
Cumulative effects theory			

All of them.

1 No answer is given for this question.

2 If a narrow idea of what is attractive is repeated across media forms and products over a period of time, audiences may interpret this idea of 'beauty' as being normal or natural. This way of thinking rejects alternative definitions of attractiveness. Audience members who compare themselves to this 'normal' idea of attractiveness may feel they are failing to live up to the ideal and, for some individuals, this could impact on their self-esteem and may impact on the behaviour.

The media can have an impact on the way people **learn about the norms and values of the surrounding culture**. Along with family, friends and education the media can impact on the socialisation of a person. The media reproduces the norms about the producing culture and these values become part of the way a person **learns to behave and interact with others**. This is called the mainstreaming process. Social roles and norms are standardised in media representations. The media cultivates attitudes and values that fit in with the dominant ideologies of the culture.

Hartley and Fiske argue that the media has a bardic function for audiences **acting to tell the stories that help communicate the fears, concerns and preoccupations of the producing culture**. Media products also generate their own 'realities'. Studies showed that **the more a person accessed the media, the more they absorbed the ideas being communicated**. The difference between light users and heavy users is called the cultivation differential. Where messages in the media **relate to the audience's experiences** they are said to have resonance This allows the mainstreaming of these ideas. This is the process that means that **heavy media users from different social groups tend to have a similar world view** that reflects the views communicated across the media. Often the ideas communicated by the media are very negative. **People often think the world is a more dangerous and violent place than it really is**. This is called the mean world index.

1 Answers for two are given below.

Media form	Interaction with producers	Interaction with audience members
Newspapers	Audience members can write letters to the editor; audience members are encouraged to phone in with information for stories.	The newspapers themselves do not offer this but it is possible for audience members to discuss stories raised in newspapers among themselves.
Radio		
Television		
Gaming	Social media offers interaction between producers and the gaming audience.	Multi-player games allow for direct interaction between players, as do forum discussion and chat opportunities connected to games sites, YouTube channels, Twitter feeds, Facebook posts, etc.
Magazines		
Film		

2 Producers can find out how audiences feel about their products and may decide to make production changes based on audience feedback. For example, the overwhelmingly negative online responses to the first half of season one of *Star Trek: Discovery* lead the writers to change direction and new plot lines were introduced in the more positively received second half of the season.

3 Audience members may use other people's opinions to frame their interpretation of a media product. Valued others and opinion leaders can influence other people's viewpoints. This can happen in person (e.g. watching TV with others) or online (e.g. reading Twitter responses to a television broadcast).

Answers for two are given below.

Media form	Contributions to media products	Creation of their own media products
Newspapers		
Radio	Audience members are the 'content' in radio phone-in programmes.	It is possible to use mobile phones and free apps to create podcasts that can be hosted on podcast sites and blogs, etc.
Television		
Gaming		
Magazines	Some magazines ask for contributions from readers that may include ideas for stories, photographs (e.g. 'street-style' images), etc.	It is possible to create blogs, vlogs and social media accounts based on any of the topics that are traditionally covered by magazines. Many Instagram accounts are modern versions of lifestyle or specialist magazines. Audiences can create beauty, fashion and general lifestyle blogs/social media accounts or could focus on specialised topics such as knitting, fitness, cooking, etc.
Film		

Model	Meaning	British example
The commercial model	Income is generated by selling space or time to advertisers.	ITV, Sky, commercial radio, YouTube, Spotify
The public service model	Income is provided by the government and is funded by citizens.	The BBC
The mixed model (commercial and public service)	Some income is provided by the government. Funds are also generated by selling advertising space.	Channel 4
The subscription model	Income is generated by audience members paying a regular (often monthly) fee to allow them to access content.	Netflix, Amazon Prime, YouTube Premium, Spotify Premium
The 'pay-per-view' model	A fee is paid to access specific content.	Sky Sports

1 No answer is given for this question.

2 Answers for two are given below.

Media form	Income streams
Film	YouTube income from trailers. Box office ticket sales, sales of merchandise and licensing agreements, sales of DVDs/Blu-Rays, sales of downloads, fees generated by streaming/TV broadcasting.
Newspapers	Advertising, cover price, promotional articles/advertorials, sponsorship. Further income can be generated by encouraging the audience to access the online newspaper and social media.
Magazines	
Online magazines/ news sites	
Computer games	
Radio	

3 Diversification allows media industries access to more and different income opportunities. Diversification also allows the industry better opportunities to find larger and broader audiences who may have differing preferences in terms of how they access media products.

Targeted advertising can only take place where an audience member's online activity is tracked and the information about their activities and interests is used (often sold) to allow advertisers to target them more specifically. This tracking is an example of **surveillance**, which raises questions about the lack of **privacy** experienced by people online. Information about what they search for is 'mined' and used to make money. Data-mining raises a number of **security** concerns as the data that are collected can be packaged and sold. User agreements often have clauses that people are not aware of. Facebook was shown recently to have accessed the phone books of users as part of the data-gathering 'agreement' that was accepted by users. There have been several examples of companies who had gathered information only to have had the data hacked.

a **Production** is ... the creation of media products.
b **Distribution** is ... getting the media product to the audience.
c **Circulation** is ... attempting to get the product in front of as many people as possible.

Answers for two are given below.

Media form	Production differences
Magazines	Lower print production values and/or a more limited distribution. Possibly focusing on a niche audience and their interests rather than a mainstream one.
Music video	Lower production values and more likely to be filmed on location rather than in a studio. May tend to be performance based.
Newspapers	
Radio	
Television	
Gaming	

Answers for two are given below.

Form	Traditional distribution methods	Benefits for the audience and/or producer	Newer distribution methods	Benefits for the audience and/or producer
Television programming	Scheduled broadcast via a television channel.	Audience can engage in live online discussions whilst watching. Industry can judge the success and reception of the product immediately.	DVD box sets, streaming services.	Audience can choose when and how they wish to watch the programme. Other methods of distribution create new income streams and can introduce the product to new audiences.
Magazines	Print magazines sold in retail outlets.	Audience can carry the magazine around with them, read it at their leisure. The magazine can be dipped into whenever the reader wishes. Industries can sell advertising space and charge a cover price for the magazine. Being on shelves in supermarkets makes the brand visible.	'Magazines' distributed as online versions (websites) and by using social media.	Audiences can access the magazine for free and the content is updated frequently. Industries can sell online advertising space and the data gathered about their audience to marketers. Producers no longer have to pay for print production and the physical distribution of the product.
Music videos				

Answers for two are given below.

a Clips from the film could be posted on YouTube and Twitter. The film could be mentioned in comments/ social media discussions surrounding similar films. A social media influencer could be approached to help promote the film by mentioning it on Instagram.

c A widespread poster campaign could be used to create awareness with the posters being posted on Twitter and other social media sites. 'Stars' of the show could make personal appearances and these could be promoted via social media.

1 IPSO: Information can be found at: www.ipso.co.uk/.

Ofcom: Information can be found at: www.ofcom.org.uk/home.

PEGI: Information can be found at: https://pegi.info/.

2 To protect children and vulnerable people from violent imagery, etc.

To protect the rights of the audience (e.g. privacy).

To ensure that the media is fair and accurate.

To maintain agreed standards of public discourse … and other arguments.

3 The amount of information online is so large that it would be impossible to impose regulation on all of it.

The internet allows easy access to material created from around the world.

Different countries have different ideas and practices regarding regulation.

Distribution is not always controlled by a media industry that can be regulated.

4 Regulation of traditional media means it cannot compete for audiences in the same ways as online and digital media.

1 **a** International conglomerates have access to all aspects of production and distribution and this means they can lower the costs of making media products and getting them to the audience.

They have access to people and technology to ensure that their product is high quality.

They can use the profits of successful products to help support more niche, less profitable products.

They can also strike deals with distributors (e.g. retail outlets) to give them a competitive edge over smaller companies.

b The BBC has a guaranteed income from the licence fee which means it is not under the same kind of financial pressures as a commercial company.

2 A limitation in the variety of messages and ideas being communicated.

Lack of competition in the market place – the audience's choices are limited.

Too much power in one place.

Two answers are given below.

Start a 'lifestyle' YouTube channel	A smartphone, tablet or computer with a video camera and an internet connection. Access to editing software could be an advantage.
Create music and upload to Soundcloud	A mobile phone, tablet or computer with a recording function and an internet connection. Access to composition, mixing and music editing software.
Create an Instagram account presenting images and ideas about health and fitness	
Create a blog on which you analyse and comment on current news and politics	

Two answers are given below.

A 'lifestyle' YouTube channel	The presenter could be featured in a magazine (on a magazine website). Collaboration videos could be created with existing influencers.
An artist whose music is available on Soundcloud	A video could be uploaded to YouTube; the artist could be interviewed by a YouTube interviewer and featured on Instagram posts.
A health and fitness-based Instagram account	
A news and politics blog	

Index